Lauri Williamson

111 Places
in Black Culture
in Washington, DC
That You Must
Not Miss

Photographs by David Wardrick

T0243792

emons:

To Carrie and Donald Nichols
for always believing in me

© Emons Verlag GmbH
All rights reserved
© Photographs by David Wardrick, except see p. 237
© Cover icon: shutterstock/Marina Podrez
Cover layout: Karolin Meinert
Layout: Editorial Design & Artdirection, Conny Laue,
based on a design by Lübbeke | Naumann | Thoben
Maps: altancicek.design, www.altancicek.de
Basic cartographical information from Openstreetmap,
© OpenStreetMap-Mitwirkende, OdbL
Edited by: Karen E. Seiger
Printing and binding: CPI – Clausen & Bosse, Leck
Printed in Germany 2024
ISBN 978-3-7408-2003-9
First edition

Guidebooks for Locals & Experienced Travelers
Join us in uncovering new places around the world at
www.111places.com

Foreword

In Washington, DC, we see historic things happening almost every day. We have a front-row view of real events that will one day fill history books. It's exciting to visit the Supreme Court, watch Congress in session, or tour the White House. There's nothing quite like gazing up close at the majestic spires of the US Air Force Memorial or taking a stroll through East Potomac Park against the backdrop of the DC Wharf and the Japanese cherry trees. It's a delight to stumble upon outdoor plaques and markers that reveal stories that would otherwise have been lost, such as the reason there's a carousel outside the Smithsonian Castle or which tree is dedicated to Reverend Dr. Martin Luther King, Jr.

I was raised in New Jersey, and my introduction to DC happened when I attended Howard University. I first heard about Howard when reading about one of its famous graduates, Thurgood Marshall, the first African American Supreme Court Justice. Howard students are immersed in Black history and culture. I took a class on the Black diaspora and was shocked by all that I didn't know. I fell in love with DC and stayed.

I never thought I would experience such an immersion again. But when the National Museum of African American History and Culture opened in 2016, I immediately became a volunteer, working around my work schedule, and it has been one of the most rewarding experiences of my life. As a professional guide, I lead tours for school groups, corporations, and local organizations, and I try to give them the same experience that I first had at Howard by taking them to places they've never been and sharing stories they've never heard. I've aimed to do the same for you among these pages.

This book has been a gift that allows me to tell stories about individuals and places that are intertwined with the narrative of this incredible city. I hope you enjoy exploring across Washington, DC as much as I did while writing this book.

111 Places

1 A. Philip Randolph
Founding a brotherhood of extraordinary men

If you've traveled by train through Union Station, you have likely walked past the larger-than-life bronze sculpture honoring civil rights activist A. (Asa) Philip Randolph (1889 – 1979).

The Pullman Palace Car Company, founded in 1867 by Chicago businessman George Pullman, built and operated luxurious railroad sleeping cars for wealthy white travelers and provided free Black men employment opportunities. More than 20,000 Black men worked as porters at the height of luxury rail travel in the 1920s.

The excellent service the Pullman porters provided was integral to the success of the passenger railroad industry. Still, they worked 400 hours or 11,000 miles per month, whichever came first, during 20-hour shifts and with only three to four hours of sleep in between before they received their pay. They regularly endured discrimination and harassment in exchange for very low wages.

The Pullman Porters urged Randolph, a well-known socialist and publisher of the magazine *The Messenger*, to become their group's president. Randolph agreed and founded the nation's first major Black labor union, the Brotherhood of Sleeping Car Porters (BSCP) in 1925, which later included maids. BSCP eventually won a collective bargaining agreement with Pullman that recognized the union and improved worker pay and conditions.

Randolph's achievements also include convincing President Franklin D. Roosevelt to end discrimination in the nation's defense industries and helping to persuade President Harry Truman to desegregate the US Armed Forces. In 1963, with Randolph planning a march for jobs and the Reverend Dr. Martin Luther King, Jr and his Southern Christian Leadership Conference (SCLC) planning one for freedom, the two groups merged their efforts into one mass protest. An estimated 250,000 people attended the 1963 March on Washington for Jobs and Freedom at the Lincoln Memorial.

Address Union Station, 50 Massachusetts Avenue NE, Washington, DC 20002 | Getting there Metro to Union Station (Red Line); bus 96, D6, X8 to Union Station; DC Circulator to Union Station (National Mall Line) | Hours Unrestricted | Tip In the Union Market food hall, go eat at Puddin', known for their New Orleans-style cuisine, including shrimp 'n grits, gumbo, and Brown Bourbon Butter Bread Puddin' (1309 5th Street NE, www.dcpuddin.com).

2 Alethia Tanner Park

A persevering spirit

The modern, 2.5-acre Alethia Tanner Park celebrates the tenacity, ingenuity, and resilience of Alethia Browning Tanner (1781–1864), who was born enslaved. She would go on to buy her own freedom in 1810 and eventually the freedom of more than 20 family members and neighbors.

Tanner was born in Prince George's County, Maryland and eventually moved to Washington, DC. Not much is known about her immediate family except that she had two sisters, Sophia and Laurena. At some point, she married a man by the name of Jeremiah Tanner but did not have any children with him. Tanner grew vegetables and ran a produce stand during the late 1700s and early 1800s on the public grounds in front of the White House at President's Park, which is now known as Lafayette Square. She purchased her freedom in 1810 with $1,400 she had earned and saved. She may have also performed some work for Thomas Jefferson at the White House during his presidency from 1801–1809.

Once free, Tanner and her extended family founded churches and schools to promote Black communities and education, continuing the work they had begun in uplifting the lives of others. She was also a founding member of Black institutions that still exist today, including today's Metropolitan AME Church on M Street, formerly Union Bethel Church, for which she co-owned the mortgage at one time. She would have been a witness to history in the city when President Abraham Lincoln signed into law the Compensated Emancipation Act on April 16, 1862, officially ending slavery in Washington, DC. The first piece of legislation to lead towards the abolition of slavery, it resulted in the liberation of over 3,000 Black people.

The community park has tables and chairs for relaxing and play areas for children of all ages, including a maze of mirrors to walk through and lots of fun structures to climb on.

Address 227 Harry Thomas Way NE, Washington, DC 20002, www.nomaparks.org |
Getting there Metro to Noma-Gallaudet University (Red Line); bus P6 to R & 2nd Street NE,
or bus 90, 92 to Florida Avenue & Eckington Place NE | Hours Daily dawn–dusk | Tip Get fit
with Wired Wellness, where you can improve mind, body, and spirit through group cycling,
mindfulness and yoga classes, and private coaching (2028 4th Street NE, www.wiredwellbeing.com).

3 Alma Thomas Home
A place of inspiration for 70 years

Alma Woodsey Thomas (1891–1978) was the first Black woman to have her artwork added to the permanent art collection in the White House. Former President and First Lady Barack and Michelle Obama added Thomas' *Resurrection,* a brightly colored abstract painting completed in 1966, to the Family Dining Room.

Thomas was born in Columbus, Georgia. Her parents moved the family to Washington, DC in 1907 to escape racial violence in the South and to have access to better schools in DC's Shaw neighborhood, a center for Black education. The art classes she was able to take in school had a profound impact on her life. Thomas once said, "When I entered the art room, it was like entering heaven... the Armstrong High School laid the foundation for my life."

In 1924, Thomas was the first graduate of Howard University's newly formed Art Department. It is widely held that she was the first Black woman in the country to receive a degree in fine arts. From 1925 to 1960, Thomas taught at Shaw Junior High School, while continuing her painting and studies. She studied at American University and earned a master's degree in art from Columbia University in the early 1930s.

Thomas is remembered for her impact on the art world. In 1972, at the age of 81, she became the first Black woman to have a solo show at the Whitney Museum in New York City, one of the most renowned art museums in the world. In an interview with *The New York Times*, Thomas recalled the fact that Black Americans had no access to cultural institutions when she lived in Columbus as a child. "One of the things we couldn't do was go into museums, let alone think of hanging our pictures there," she said. "My, times have changed. Just look at me now."

Thomas is significant not only for her artistic contributions, but also for her dedication to educating and introducing both young and adult African Americans to the world of art.

Address 1530 15th Street NW, Washington, DC 20005, www.historicsites.dcpreservation.org |
Getting there Metro to McPherson Square (Blue, Orange, Silver Lines), then walk 12 minutes;
bus S2 to 16th & Q Streets NW; DC Circulator to 14th Street & Rhode Island Avenue NW
(Woodley Park Metro Line) | Hours Unrestricted from the outside only | Tip Georgia Johnson
Douglas was the author of four books of poems, six plays, and 32 song lyrics, making her the
best-published woman author of the Harlem Renaissance. Now a private home with a historic
marker, her house was the site of the "Saturday Nighters," a literary salon Johnson hosted from
the 1920s into the 1940s (1461 S Street NW, historicsites.dcpreservation.org).

4 Anacostia Art Gallery & Boutique

Connecting cultures for over 30 years

The Anacostia Art Gallery and Boutique is your go-to place for unique gifts. Colorful masks made from coconuts, hand carved African chairs, skincare products, and unique ceramics with tribal motifs are just some of the many items for purchase. Juanita Britton, nicknamed "Busy Bee" at the age of three by her grandmother, is as busy as ever. She is the CEO of BZB International, Inc., a public relations, event planning, and travel firm. A former diplomat, she is a master at making connections and promoting Black businesses.

She has produced the popular BZB Shop Marketplace event for more than 30 years, bringing together dozens of Black-owned brands. Shoppers come to shop from the extraordinary collections here. "Inspiration comes from producing this event with amazing artisans and designers," says Britton, who first had the idea during a visit to Brixton Market in South Central London, a street market with a variety of local artisans. She'd never seen anything like it before.

She was further inspired to find a way to help businesses continue selling their wares during the COVID-19 pandemic. Artists who frequented a bed-and-breakfast she owns suggested she turn it into retail space. That space today is the Anacostia Art Gallery & Boutique, where you can find fine art, couture clothing, collectibles, housewares, jewelry, and everything in between. "I brought that same marketplace feel into the boutique," says Britton. "It's a little bit of everything because I want to present things from many different artists."

Britton curates the items from over 75 different businesses and artisans around the world. She works with 12 women's cooperatives across Africa for jewelry and other handmade items. She believes in supporting these women, who, in turn, support their own communities. She also hosts exciting events, including art exhibits, book signings, and more.

Address 119 Raleigh Street SE, Washington, DC 20032, +1 (202) 550-7060,
www.anacostiaartgallery.com, BusyBee@anacostiaartgallery.com | Getting there Metro to
Anacostia (Green Line); bus A4 to MLK Avenue & Sterling Street SE | Hours Mar–Nov
Sat & Sun 11am–6pm | Tip For delicious, elevated comfort food visit Kitchen Savages
and try their crab cake egg rolls, wings or honey blackened salmon. And take home some
banana pudding! Winner of Washington City Paper's best new restaurant and best wings
categories (1211 Good Hope Road SE, www.kitchensavages.com).

5 Anacostia Community Museum

DC's community home for history

The Smithsonian Institution's Anacostia Museum sits on a hill overlooking the historic neighborhood of Anacostia, one of the more than 40 neighborhoods on the eastern side of the Anacostia River. Founded in 1967, the museum shares the all but untold and often overlooked stories of communities furthest from justice in the greater Washington, DC region. In celebrating stories of resilience, joy, and strength, the museum inspires those who visit to translate their ideas into actions.

The museum curates and hosts annual exhibitions that run in its main gallery, masterfully using a variety of storytelling methods, such as large-scale storyboards, video, and placement of key artifacts, to highlight the year's specific theme. The museum's staff discusses ideas and works on exhibits for several years to determine each year's focus. For 2024, the museum's exhibition is called, "A Bold and Beautiful Vision," which seeks to illuminate the long and rich tradition of Black artist-educators in the city, who inspired and who were inspired by the artistic interests of generations of young people during the 20th century. Unlike museums with several permanent exhibits, the Anacostia Community Museum reinvents itself every year.

To stay connected with the community, the museum also regularly hosts a variety of in-person events, such as Coffee and Collections, where museum artifacts are highlighted; live musical performances; and Craftivist Circle, where visitors engage in crafts while discussing societal issues of the day which are listed on the website. The FRESHFARM ACM farm stand offers fresh produce here every Saturday from April to November, weather permitting, supporting local farmers and providing opportunities to learn about cooking regional crops. All events and programming take place on one level that's easy for people with mobility challenges to navigate.

Address 1901 Fort Place SE, Washington, DC 20020, +1 (202) 633-4820, www.anacostia.si.edu |
Getting there Metro to Anacostia (Green Line), transfer to bus W2 to the 1901 Fort Place SE |
Hours Daily 10am–5pm | Tip Add some fun to your day with urban line dancing, pop, and
soul music every first and third Wednesday of the month! Learn choreographed routines in
at the DC Dream Center with Saundra Richardson, owner of Style & Rhythm Line Dancers
(2826 Q Street SE, www.dcdreamcenter.com/events).

6 Arlington National Cemetery – Section 27

Recognition at the most esteemed military cemetery

On a hilltop overlooking Washington, DC sits Arlington National Cemetery (ANC), which holds an important place in Black history. When Arlington became a national cemetery in 1864, all burials were segregated by race and military rank. Section 27 was designated an African American burial area. Segregation continued until the Military was desegregated in 1948.

During the Civil War (1861–1865), the US government recruited African Americans to serve in all-Black regiments of the Union Army, collectively called the United States Colored Troops (USCT). Close to 180,000 African Americans chose to fight for freedom, and about 1,500 of these soldiers are buried in Section 27. Their headstones are marked with a Civil War shield and the letters "USCT" or "USCI" (US Colored Infantry).

Look for the graves of three Black men who were awarded the Medal of Honor for their conduct during the Civil War: Sergeant James H. Harris (St. Mary's County, MD) of the 38th USCT and William H. Brown of the US Navy (Baltimore, MD) in Section 27, and Sergeant Milton M. Holland (Austin, TX) of the 5th USCT in Section 23.

In addition to African American military heroes, an estimated 3,000 "contrabands" – enslaved people who escaped to freedom – are also buried in Section 27. They were freed as Union forces moved south during the war or escaped from enslavement in Virginia and Maryland. Their headstones are marked "Citizen" or "Civilian."

Secretary of the Smithsonian Institution Lonnie G. Bunch III visits Section 27 every year to pay homage. "There is nothing more noble than honoring our ancestors by remembering," he states.

As you walk through Section 27 today, you can also view the restored Arlington estate house and the adjacent quarters for enslaved people.

Address Arlington National Cemetery, Arlington, VA 22211, +1 (877) 907-8585, www.arlingtoncemetery.mil | Getting there Metro to Arlington Cemetery (Blue Line) | Hours Daily 8am–5pm | Tip Explore the history of Freedman's Village in Arlington National Cemetery and the surrounding area at The Black Heritage Museum of Arlington, which celebrates the historic journey to freedom in Arlington County, Virginia (3045-B Columbia Pike, Arlington, VA, www.arlingtonblackheritage.org).

7 — Art of Noize

An intimate space to celebrate the Arts

Walking into the Art of Noize feels like you've been invited into some cool, artistic, friend-of-a-friend's living room for an intimate get together with good people, entertainment, and conversation. Owner Adrian Ferguson, an avid vinyl record collector with artistry in his family's DNA, transformed this formerly empty industrial space into a place that artists from a variety of disciplines use to showcase their talents in the local community.

"I started Art of Noize because at the time, DC really didn't have non-traditional, flexible art and creative spaces," Ferguson says. "Everything was very traditional and expensive, and I wanted to create a space that was intimate and affordable."

Ferguson defines the "noise" as music, spoken word, and acting. Not to be missed are the monthly evening "Sessions," where local artists find an engaged and supportive audience. Ferguson calls Sessions "an open mic jam session for instrumentalists, vocalists, MCs, spoken word artists, dancers – anyone willing to share their art and play, sing, rap, or dance as if no one is watching." One or two featured artists are promoted in advance, and then the evening transitions to open mic performances from members of the audience, who sign up for available spots. Step up to the cash bar and buy some snacks, and then you can settle in and enjoy some of the best art and music in town.

In addition to creating areas for performing artists, the walls here are also used as gallery spaces to showcase the work of established and emerging local artists. The rotating art exhibits are also viewable on the Art of Noize website and available for purchase.

You'll reach the gallery and performance space through an alley in the Petworth neighborhood in Northwest DC that is known for its community events and unique mix of residences and local businesses that gives it a small-town feel.

Address 821 Upshur Street NW Rear, 2nd Floor, Washington, DC 20011, www.artofnoizedmv.com, artofnoizedmv@gmail.com | Getting there Metro to Georgia Avenue-Petworth (Green Line), then walk nine minutes; bus 60, 62, 63, 70, 78 to Georgia Avenue & Upshur Street NW | Hours Thu–Sat noon–6pm | Tip Stop in at the Little Food Studio (LFS) Café for a breakfast pastry and coffee, a quick sandwich for lunch, or one of their refreshing specialty lemonades. Watch Chef Danielle on *Secret Chef* season one streaming on Hulu (849 Upshur Street NW, www.littlefoodstudio.com).

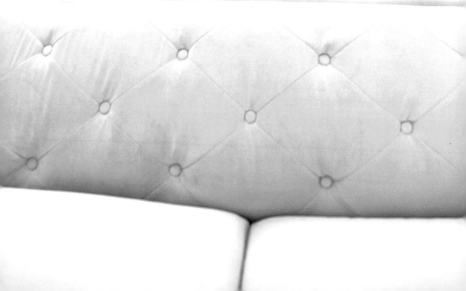

8 Asbury UMC
Witness to history

Asbury United Methodist Church (UMC) was founded in 1836 under the leadership of Eli Nugent, who led a group of congregants from Foundry Methodist Episcopal Church to found their own church after experiencing racial discrimination. Asbury is the oldest Black church in DC that still stands on its original site. The current Gothic Revival style building features an open truss ceiling made of wooden beams and beautiful stained-glass windows.

The church and its congregation have played an active role in the city's history through abolition, emancipation, reconstruction, and the civil rights movement. Notable congregants and active members of the church have included Mary Church Terrell and Mary McLeod Bethune. Warm and welcoming Sunday services include a sermon, along with choirs performing a variety of music styles.

In 1947, the church established the first interracial housing facility in the nation's capital, which today provides shelter for the aged and disabled. They later established the Asbury Federal Credit Union, the first of its kind in any church in DC.

On December 12, 2020, the church experienced a hate crime when their Black Lives Matter banner was burned on the church grounds. The attack made national headlines, and one week later, a new banner installed was stolen. Today, another banner stands proudly in front of the church. "We are a people of faith. As horrible and disturbing as this is for us now, it doesn't compare with the challenges and fears the men and women who started Asbury 184 years ago faced," said senior pastor Rev. Dr. Ianther M. Mills in a statement referenced on the church's website. "We believe this is a wakeup call for all to be more vigilant and committed to anti-racism and building a beloved community, and we invite you to join us. Our congregation will continue to stand steadfast – 'we will not be moved.'"

926 11th Street NW, Washington, DC 20001, +1 (202) 628-0009, www.asburyumcdc.org, asburymail@asburyumcdc.org   Metro to McPherson Square (Blue, Orange, Silver Lines); bus 63, 64, G8 to 11th & K Streets NW; DC Circulator to 13th & K Streets NW (Georgetown-Union Station Line)   See website for services and events   The Metropolitan AME Church, the oldest African Methodist Episcopal church in DC, harbored runaway freedom seekers, supported AIDS education, and holds voter registration projects today. Funeral services for Frederick Douglass and former US Senator Blanche K. Bruce were held here (1518 M Street NW, www.metropolitaname.org).

9 Banneker Ballroom Dance Club

Dancing is a shortcut to happiness

"Ballroom dance" is an umbrella term to describe partner dances such as the waltz, rhumba, foxtrot, tango, and swing, as well as DC hand dance, DC's official dance derived from the Lindy Hop which was created by Black dancers during the Harlem Renaissance during the 1920s and 1930s.

The first classes of the Banneker Ballroom Dance Club (BBDC) were held in the 1940s at the Banneker Recreation Center, a popular recreational spot in the city for African Americans in a time of segregation. According to the BBDC website, the classes included not only instruction in proper dance technique, but also on proper dress, etiquette, and deportment. Every man attending a Banneker dance class had to wear a necktie.

The club held its first banquet at Waters' Catering Service in Rockville, Maryland. About 29 elegantly attired attendees brightened the evening. This event started a tradition of galas with over 250 attendees and dance exhibitions that continue around the DC area today. Classes today are "come as you are." It is important to wear comfortable clothing and shoes with leather soles or dance sneakers that allow you to move and turn easily. All are welcome to attend classes, and you don't need to bring a partner. Women and men learn dance steps separately and are then partnered so that they learn how to dance with partners. It's great fun, and people do "dress to impress" for social dances and galas.

Ballroom Club president Brenda Manley says, "The elegance of ballroom is a dance form we strive to keep healthy and alive within the African American community. Through professional instruction, affordability, and energetic organization the vibrance and tradition of ballroom continues to be a gem of Washington, DC dance culture."

Address 6310 Chillum Place NW, Washington, DC 20011, www.bannekerballroomdance.com, +1 (202) 256-7218, banneker_info@bannekerballroomdance.com | Getting there Metro to Takoma (Red Line), transfer to bus F1 to Eastern Avenue & N Capitol Street NE | Hours Check website for class schedule | Tip Be a part of the health movement at Turning Natural, which features juices, cleanses, smoothies and food. No artificial coloring, no ice, no syrups, no flavorings, no sugar – just the good stuff... and love (6833 4th Street NW, www.turningnatural.com).

10 __ Ben's Chili Bowl
Eat like a King

Ben and Virginia Ali opened Ben's Chili Bowl on August 22, 1958, and it became popular as a welcoming gathering place for the community almost immediately. Ben's is home to DC's signature dish, chili hot dogs and half smokes served on warm, steamed buns. They are best enjoyed the original way with mustard, onions, and Ben's homemade spicy chili sauce.

For the uninitiated, half smokes are sausages that are usually smoked before being grilled. They're often a bit spicier than a hot dog and made from meat that's more coarsely ground. Ben's expanded menu offers burgers, chicken, and homemade desserts, along with vegetarian and vegan options. Pull up to one of their signature red barstools or find a seat in the back room amidst the celebrity photos. Dr. Martin Luther King, Jr. was a customer here, even during the weekend when he delivered his famous "I Have a Dream" speech. Dr. King's go-to meal? The chili cheeseburger.

Ben's owners have always cared about the community, serving people and donating food during countless events, such as the March on Washington and the Poor People's Campaign, and to frontline personnel during the COVID-19 pandemic. Every five years in August, Ben's holds a celebratory event. "I was definitely overwhelmed with joy when we celebrated our 65th anniversary in 2023, and I saw so many people crowding out in that hot sun, it was just wonderful," remembers Mrs. Ali. "And we weren't giving anything away! I had no idea that we had that much love and support."

When you eat at Ben's, you not only get good food, but you also become part of a legacy that helps fuel community spirit. The Ben's Chili Bowl Foundation supports schools and community organizations and continues the legacy of giving back that the Alis began in 1958. "We have the respect of the community, and I think that's the most important thing of all," says Mrs. Ali.

Address 1213 U Street NW, Washington, DC 20009, +1 (202) 667-0909, www.benschilibowl.com, hello@benschilibowl.com | Getting there Metro to U Street/African American Civil War Memorial/Cardozo (Green Line); bus 90, 92, 96 13th & U Streets NW; DC Circulator to 14th & U Streets NW (Woodley Park-Adams Morgan-McPherson Square Line) | Hours Mon–Wed 11am–9pm, Thu 11am–11pm, Fri & Sat 11am–4am, Sun 11am–10pm | Tip Lee's flower shop, a trusted, family-owned business that has been serving the community since 1945, is the oldest Black-owned flower shop in DC and possibly the nation (1026 U Street NW, www.leesflowerandcard.com).

11   Black Lives Matter Plaza

Proof that truth still marches on

Looking south while standing at 16th and K Streets NW gives you a direct view of the White House. However, that view now includes a display of bright yellow letters spanning two city blocks that boldly spell out BLACK LIVES MATTER.

George Floyd of Minnesota and Breonna Taylor of Kentucky were not the first Black Americans who lost their lives due to police brutality or racial injustice, but their deaths in 2020 were pivotal in escalating massive civil unrest around the globe. On June 1, 2020, people across the globe were shocked to see reports of peaceful demonstrators facing violence and tear gas from federal officials near this protest site.

On June 5, Mayor Muriel Bowser commissioned the art installation and unveiled Black Lives Matter Plaza to the city and the world. She said at the unveiling ceremony, "There are people craving to be heard and to be seen and to have their humanity recognized."

The plaza was immediately controversial. Following the opening, vandals spray-painted at least half a dozen expletive-laden messages against law enforcement, the mayor, and the art. While some felt the plaza made an important statement, others felt it only gave lip service to important issues facing Blacks in an increasingly gentrifying city. And yet many consider it a place for the community to come together for open expression and healing.

Civil rights pioneer Congressman John Lewis visited the plaza shortly before his death. "I just had to see and feel it for myself that, after many years of silent witness, the truth is still marching on," Lewis wrote in *The New York Times*.

Black Lives Matter Plaza was completed and declared a permanent installation in October 2021. The street has reopened to offer limited passage by vehicles, and updates continue to make it a more cohesive public space with commemorative works, benches, lighting, signage, and trees.

Address 16th Street NW between K & H Streets NW, Washington, DC 20006, www.washington.org/visit-dc/black-lives-matter-plaza | Getting there Metro to McPherson Square (Blue, Orange, Silver Lines); bus 32, 33, 36, 11Y, G8, to H Street & Madison Place NW; DC Circulator to K & 16th Streets NW (Georgetown-Union Station Line) | Hours Unrestricted | Tip In nearby Lafayette Square, a series of markers recount the history of the involvement of enslaved labor in the construction, preservation, and commemoration of the White House and Lafayette Square itself (1601 Pennsylvania Avenue NW, www.whitehousehistory.org).

12 Blagden Alley/ Naylor Court

Hidden history in a living museum

Blagden Alley/Naylor Court is a posh and historic neighborhood destination. Today, you can stroll through the area and enjoy trendy restaurants, coffee shops, and an open-air "alley museum" of colorful and thought-provoking murals. Beautiful homes in Federal, Italianate, and other styles dating from about 1833 to 1941 are interspersed with million-dollar condos. But within the the alleys lics an unexpected history of life in early Washington, DC. Life here was once very different.

The city once had hundreds of interconnected alleyways to provide access to buildings or animals. The two-block Blagden Alley/Naylor Court lots were included in the original city plan laid out by Pierre L'Enfant in 1791. They represent the best architectural example of the city's few remaining alley communities. Black people migrated to the capital in large numbers during and after the Civil War, and many who were formerly enslaved found shelter in alley dwellings that were small and poorly constructed. The alleys were overcrowded, unsafe, and unsanitary, but they were the only homes available for many families, who were able to create a sense of community even under those conditions. The area also included a small number of working-class white people, service shops, metal works, and stables. In his book *Alley Life in Washington: Family, Community, Religion, and Folklife in the City, 1850-1970* James Borchert reports that the number of alley dwellers was nearly 19,000 in 1897.

Efforts to abolish alley dwellings by the government and social campaigns began in the early 1900s. By the 1960s, those with enough resources fled to the suburbs, and the 1968 riots resulted in abandonment of the alley dwellings and street-facing properties. Based on the work of residents, Blagden Alley/Naylor Court was designated a historic district in 1990.

Address Blagden Alley NW, Washington, DC 20001, +1 (202) 783-5144, historicsites. dcpreservation.org, info@dcpreservation.org | Getting there Metro to Mount Vernon Square-7th Street (Green, Yellow Lines); bus G8 to 9th & N Streets NW, or bus 63, 64, G8 to 11th & N Streets NW; DC Circulator to 9th Street & New York Avenue NW (Georgetown-Union Station Line) | Hours Unrestricted | Tip See Duke Ellington's birth certificate and the original wills of historical figures, including Frederick Douglass, Alexander Graham Bell, and Oliver Wendell Holmes at the District Archives, located in an 88-year-old former horse barn (1300 Naylor Court NW, www.os.dc.gov).

13 Blanche Kelso Bruce Home

From slavery to the Senate

This red, second empire-style house was the home of Blanche Kelso Bruce (1841–1898). A plaque on the fence outside reveals the story behind this National Historic Landmark. Bruce was the first Black person to serve a full term in the United States Senate. He also broke new ground as registrar of the Treasury in 1881, thereby being the first Black person with his signature on US currency.

Bruce was born in Prince Edward County, Virginia in 1841 to his enslaved mother Polly Bruce. Her enslaver was also Bruce's father. Bruce learned to read and write in his youth alongside his white half-brother. At eight years old, he was forced to pick cotton and subjected to cruel treatment. In 1862, he escaped to Kansas, and, later in 1864, he established the first school for Black children in the State of Missouri.

Bruce moved on to Mississippi in 1869 during Reconstruction and became a member of the Republican Party. Smart and politically shrewd, he was appointed conductor of elections for Tallahatchie County and later served as superintendent of education for Bolivar County. Bruce was elected to the US Senate in 1875, where he would be a strong advocate for political reform in federal elections. He also spoke out for civil rights for Blacks, and especially for veterans, Native Americans, and Chinese immigrants.

In 1878, Bruce married the elegant and beautiful Josephine Willson, daughter of a prominent Cleveland dentist. The couple were leaders of Washington's Black aristocracy, and their home became a center of social life. Josephine helped found the National Association of Colored Women in 1896, and, in 1899, she joined the staff at Tuskegee Institute in Alabama. Their only child, Roscoe Conkling Bruce (1879–1950), graduated Phi Beta Kappa from Harvard in 1902 and became an educator. He later served as editor-in-chief of the Harriet Tubman Publishing Company.

Address 909 M Street NW, Washington, DC 20001, +1 (202) 783-5144, historicsites.dcpreservation.org, info@dcpreservation.org | **Getting there** Metro to Mount Vernon Square/7th Street-Convention Center (Yellow, Green Lines); bus G8 to 9th & N Streets NW | **Hours** Unrestricted from the outside only | **Tip** Take a public tour of a $6.5-million-dollar art collection featuring many local artists and culturally diverse works at the Walter E. Washington Convention Center a block away (801 Allen Y. Lew Place NW, https://eventsdc.com/venue/walter-e-washington-convention-center).

14 Blues Alley Jazz
Dizzy's ongoing legacy

The city of Washington, DC is in constant flux, but the legendary Blues Alley Jazz supper club has thankfully remained the same. The club was established in 1965 in an old carriage house, and you can still find its entrance in an alley off of Wisconsin Avenue in Georgetown. Nicknamed "The House That Dizzy Built" after internationally renowned jazz trumpeter Dizzy Gillespie, Blues Alley is the nation's oldest continually operating jazz supper club. It's a great place to go solo on your own, on a date night, or an evening out with friends and fellow music lovers.

Seating is intimate, and you can find a spot close to the stage, or you can sit further back towards the bar. The menu is Creole, featuring dishes like jambalaya, shrimp and grits, and red beans and rice. You can also opt for shareable plates, like chips with spinach and artichoke dip or fried chicken wings.

Most importantly, you'll enjoy some of the best live music performances in the city, featuring musicians who travel to DC from around the world. There are two shows per night, seven nights per week where you can hear jazz, blues, soul, Big Band, or R&B. The ticket price comes with a moderate minimum purchase requirement, and seating is first come, first served.

What most locals don't know is that in 1985, Blues Alley and Dizzy Gillespie founded the Blues Alley Jazz Society, a non-profit organization "dedicated to the enlightenment of our youth, and the promotion of jazz music through education," according to the Blues Alley website. The Society formed the Blues Alley Youth Orchestra in 1985 for accomplished local student musicians ranging in age from 13 to 18 years old. Orchestra members take part in both civic and educational opportunities, performing in senior centers, at community functions, and inside houses of worship. Auditions for the youth orchestra are open year round.

Address 1073 Wisconsin Avenue NW, Washington, DC 20007, +1 (202) 337-4141, www.bluesalley.com, communications@bluesalley.com | Getting there Metro to Foggy Bottom (Blue, Orange, Silver Lines); bus 31, 33, 38B to M Street Wisconsin Avenue & NW; DC Circulator to Wisconsin Avenue & M Street NW (Georgetown-Union Station Line) | Hours Daily 6–11pm | Tip The City Tavern in Georgetown is the last remaining Federal tavern in DC (c. 1796). The historic site offers lectures, guided tours, and social and cultural events highlighting the tavern's story, its historical relationship with slavery, and its 18th-century architecture and interiors (3206 M Street NW, www.citytavernc.org).

15 Button Farm

Oprah's training ground

Tony Cohen is founder and director of the Menare Foundation that works to preserve the legacy of the Underground Railroad (UGRR). He's a historian and the visionary behind the Button Farm Living History Center, Maryland's only venue that depicts 19th-century plantation life. "Visitors get a sensory experience of plantation life and the story of the Underground Railroad through our guided tours of the farm and the landscape of the 6,000-acre park in which we operate," explains Cohen.

Button Farm was not a part of the UGRR, but you will learn about life during the 1800s and experiences on the "freedom train." Cohen knows that history better than most. In 1996, he embarked on a 1,200-mile journey from Maryland to Canada to recreate the path of the self-liberators. "I walked 8 weeks, 10–25 miles per day and only used the methods used at the time. So, by foot mainly, but also in places by boat or train." His experiences caught the attention of Oprah Winfrey, whom Cohen prepared for her role in the movie *Beloved (*1998) by creating an immersive UGRR experience at Button Farm in 1997.

The farm includes a late 19th-century barn, along with an heirloom garden growing the same kinds of crops that would be found in Montgomery County during the 1850s. You'll also encounter American guinea hogs, thought to have been bred from hogs brought over in the late 18th century from West Africa. You'll see implements that enslaved people used for farm work and view a burial ground for the enslaved.

Button Farm is open Spring through Fall, and all tours and experiences are outdoors. Cohen recommends that you make note of four special celebration days at the farm: Montgomery County Heritage days in June, the countywide farm tour in July, Tubman Day in September, and the Maryland Emancipation Day celebration held the last weekend in October.

Address 16820 Black Rock Road, Germantown, MD 20874, +1 (202) 903-4140, www.buttonfarm.org, info@buttonfarm.org | Getting there By car, take I-270 N to exit 15B, continue on MD-118 S/Germantown Road, and turn right onto Black Rock Road | Hours See website for seasonal hours and events | Tip Visit the Northampton Slave Quarters and Archeological Park in Prince George's County, Maryland to see the rebuilt foundations of two slave quarters and learn about the lives of enslaved people who resided there (10915 Water Port Court, Bowie, MD, www.experienceprincegeorges.com).

16 C&O Canal

DC's historic waterway

The Chesapeake & Ohio Canal, more commonly referred to as the C&O Canal, is a visually stunning, 184.5-mile waterway that runs from Washington, DC to Cumberland in the mountains of western Maryland. Construction of the canal began in 1828, and it operated primarily between 1850 and 1924 to transfer goods to community markets.

Laborers who built the canal included Irish immigrants, Germans, and native-born Americans, and many free and enslaved African Americans early on. Most of their stories were not recorded, but it is known that hundreds of young Black men between the ages of 18 and 25 worked on the canal as part of the Civilian Conservation Corps (CCC), tasked with building America's national parks. A lesser-known fact about the history of the canal is that it was used by freedom seekers on the Underground Railroad. One such person was 21-year-old Ben Addison, who fled along the canal during the Christmas season of 1829 after working on the canal for 3 months. As reported by the Maryland State Archives, a runaway ad offering a $50 reward for his return then ran for a month in a Frederick County newspaper.

Today, the C&O Canal National Historical Park (NHP) encompasses 20,000 acres of land and serves as a unique place to visit and appreciate nature. A historic towpath is available for walking, hiking, and biking, or you can venture further out to explore charming canal towns in Maryland or Virginia.

NPS works with the C&O Canal Trust to maintain the park, which is currently undergoing restoration expected to run through the end of 2025. While the project is underway, some portions may be affected, but there are still activities and events to enjoy during spring and summer months. And when the canal is fully restored, you can look forward to the addition of boat rides offering peaceful journeys along the watered sections of the towpath.

Address 1057 Thomas Jefferson Street NW, Washington, DC 20007, +1 (240) 202-2625, www.canaltrust.org, info@canaltrust.org | Getting there Bus 31, 33, 38B to M Street & Thomas Jefferson Street NW; DC Circulator to Wisconsin & M Streets NW (Georgetown-Union Station Line) | Hours Unrestricted | Tip Find your next favorite outfit at Everard's Clothing, a family run business that, according to their website. outfits some of the world's most prestigious men and women (1802 Wisconsin Avenue NW, www.everardsclothing.com).

17 __ Canimals! at Eastern Market

Can-tastic art for your home

Eastern Market is one of the few public market buildings left in DC. Designated as a National Historic Landmark, it has operated continuously since 1873. A variety of vendors sell everything from artwork and clothing to food and flowers, making the building and the indoor and outdoor market a fun weekend destination.

On most weekends at the outdoor market, you'll find Manatho Shumba Masani, an artist at heart, who left his Post Office job to pursue his passion. Masani makes handcrafted sculptures that he calls Canimals! He uses soda cans, beer cans, or basically any kind of can and wire to create his irresistible sculptures that have personalities all their own. His handcrafted, up-cycled giraffes are some of his most popular pieces. They are majestic, graceful, and colorful, and they can range in size from petite enough to adorn a favorite spot on your desk or coffee table to 10 feet tall. According to Masani, each one is different and carries its own unique spirit. Customers are especially attracted to the Canimals! made with Arizona tea cans because of the beautiful colors. He also sells a variety of different items, such as handmade musical instruments, clothing, and fragrances.

"Why giraffes?" you may ask? Masani responds with his favorite joke, "Giraffes make the best friends because they always stick their necks out for you." He says that giraffes are the most recognizable animals on the planet. They have the biggest hearts of any land mammal, and so they represent unconditional love.

"In Zimbabwe, the giraffe goes by the name Twiza (twee'zah), which means, 'He who grazes from the Heavens,'" says Masani. "Their long necks and keen eyesight are powerful symbols for seeing what's coming ahead." Masani's mission is to clean up the world one can at a time to create a culture of no waste by infusing inspiration with recycled materials.

Address 225 7th Street SE, Washington, DC 20003, +1 (202) 698-5253, www.easternmarketdc.org |
Getting there Metro to Eastern Market (Blue, Orange, Silver Lines); bus 90, 92 to 8th Street
& Independence Avenue SE; DC Circulator to Pennsylvania Avenue & 7th Street SE
(Eastern Market-L'Enfant Plaza Line) | Hours See website for indoor and outdoor market hours |
Tip "The Big Chair" reaches 20' tall and was created as advertising for a furniture company.
Due to deterioration of the wood, the chair has been replaced by a metal replica and has served
as a community landmark in historic Anacostia since 1959 (Martin Luther King, Jr. Avenue
& V Street SE, www.boundarystones.org).

18 Carnegie Library
The city's first integrated building

Have you ever wondered about the lone and beautiful beaux-arts building that inhabits the entire block across the street from the convention center? The building was the city's main public library from 1903–1972 and was the first desegregated public building in DC. A Carnegie library, it followed the best modern library practices at the time, with reading rooms that separated patrons by age and areas of interest. But, most notably, it did not separate patrons by race, even though most activities in the city were segregated. It now houses a historic photo gallery and the DC History Center, along with a flagship Apple store.

The gallery on the lower level gives the full history of the building, which was a gift to the citizens of Washington, DC from philanthropist Andrew Carnegie. You'll find over a dozen historic photos and a reproduced map of the 1800 city plan. Inscriptions on the interior and exterior of the building support Carnegie's ideal that education through sciences and humanities should be available to all, regardless of social status. The top level houses the DC History Center and its public exhibits, the Kiplinger Research Library, a small gift shop, and a photographic timeline of Washington, DC. The timeline begins as early as 1600 with the Nacotchtank tribe, who lived mainly along what's now the Anacostia River. Look for rotating exhibits that focus on diverse aspects of DC's history.

A decade prior to the library's construction, this location was home to a noisy and smelly Northern Liberty Market. It had also been the location of a notorious and violent riot in 1857. Residents urged then-city governor Alexander "Boss" Shepherd (1835–1902) to tear it down. He agreed, but he conducted the demolition overnight and in secret so that market vendors could not protest, and two people were killed when the walls of the two-story building suddenly came down on them.

Address 801 K Street NW, Washington, DC 20001, www.dchistory.org/about/carnegielibrary, info@dchistory.org | Getting there Metro to Mt Vernon Square (Green, Yellow Lines) or Gallery Place (Green, Yellow, Red Lines); bus 70, 79, 74 to 7th & L Streets NW, or bus P6, 80, X2, X9 to 7th & H Streets NW; DC Circulator to Massachusetts Avenue & 7th Street NW (Georgetown-Union Station Line) | Hours Thu & Fri noon–7pm, Sat & Sun noon–6pm | Tip Nearby Saints Paradise Cafeteria is a hidden gem for reasonably priced soul food. Enter under the red awning attached to the left side of the beautiful temple of the United House of Prayer for All People (601 M Street NW, Suite A).

19 Carter G. Woodson Memorial Park

Paying homage to the father of Black history

Nestled in the heart of the Shaw neighborhood on a small, triangular block sits a memorial to Dr. Carter G. Woodson (1875–1950), acclaimed historian, author, and professor known as the Father of Black History. The location is fitting, as Woodson lived and worked in this community between 1922 and 1950, where the local school children referred to him as "Bookman," since he was often seen throughout the neighborhood carrying stacks of books that he published and shipped to schools across the nation. The memorial depicts Dr. Woodson in bronze, seated and ready to chat with visitors. Depicted at the back of the memorial is a bookshelf showcasing many of the books he wrote.

The fourth of nine children born to formerly enslaved parents in Canton, VA, Woodson worked as a sharecropper and a miner to help his family. He began high school at the age of 20 and completed a four-year course of study in less than two years. Woodson earned degrees at Berea College in Kentucky and the University of Chicago in Illinois. In 1912, he would become the second Black person to earn a PhD from Harvard University. He served as dean of the School of Liberal Arts at Howard University and founded the Association for the Study of African American Life and History in 1915. It continues to operate today with branches across the US.

Woodson spent many hours researching and writing historical narratives on Black life. His most recognized book is *The Mis-Education of the Negro*, asserting the importance of the accurate retelling of Black history.

In 1926, Woodson lobbied for a week-long public celebration called Negro History Week. February was chosen because it was the birth month of Frederick Douglass and Abraham Lincoln. Through the efforts of Black students, the program was later expanded and officially recognized in 1976 as a month-long celebration each year in February.

Address 900 Rhode Island Avenue NW, Washington, DC 20001, www.nps.gov | Getting there Metro to Shaw-Howard U (Green Line); bus 70, 79 to 7th Street & Rhode Island Avenue NW | Hours Unrestricted | Tip Just a few blocks away is the Shaw Community Mural on 9th Street between P and Q Streets featuring Carter G. Woodson, Langston Hughes, Shaw Jr. High School, and Robert Gould Shaw, after whom the neighborhood is named (1507 9th Street NW, www.muralsdcproject.com).

FATHER OF
BLACK HISTORY

20 ChocCity Cornhole
Take your best shot

Cornhole is a fun game in which players toss bean bags into holes in an angled board to score points. It's become so wildly popular that Olympic rumors have been noted in the media. When that day comes, DC will be ready, thanks to Chocolate City Cornhole (ChocCity).

Jessica Davis started ChocCity to introduce underrepresented groups, mainly women of color (WOC) and queer people of color (QPOC) to the game. "When I first started playing, I quickly noticed that there weren't many people who looked like me, which sometimes affected how I showed up and played," Davis shared. "As a queer Black woman, I am aware of the spaces around me and the spaces in which I feel most comfortable. I wanted to create a comfortable, welcoming space for WOC and QPOC to come and build a community around the game of Cornhole. I also started the group because I want to create a team of skilled Cornhole players that play competitively. We are on our way!"

Davis further explains that cornhole is accessible to those facing physical and mental challenges. It can take time to master, but pretty much anyone of any age or ability can become good or skilled with practice. She hopes to begin youth groups in the future so that the next generation of players can start honing their skills.

When the group began, only five or so people would show up to play per session. This was discouraging to Davis, who thought that perhaps the interest wasn't there. Thanks to her persistence, by the end of the year, the entire 10-week winter season was maxed out with 20 – 24 players per night. A beautiful and unexpected side effect Davis has witnessed is that those participating have fostered new connections and friendships.

Participation is free, and all are welcome. And true to current culture, if you want to stay in the know and sign up for a session, you need to follow the group on Instagram @choccitycornhole.

3400 Georgia Avenue NW, Washington, DC 20010, www.choccitycornhole.com, info@choccitycornhole.com   Metro to Georgia Avenue-Petworth (Green Line); bus 70 to Georgia Avenue & Park Road NW   See website for events schedule   Negril Jamaican Eatery, founded in 1979 by Jamaican native Earl Chinn, is a favorite spot for locals who love the jerk chicken and beef patties, but everything here is delicious. Try the curried chicken or shrimp with plantains (2301 Georgia Avenue NW, Suite G, www.negrileats.com).

21 Chuck Brown Memorial Park

The official music of Washington, DC

Chuck Brown (1936–2012) is the originator of Go-Go, and Chuck Brown Memorial Park was created to honor him in larger-than-life fashion. Go-Go is a highly percussive style of dance music rooted in Latin, funk, blues, soul, and gospel music that also pulls from African rhythms. Call-and-response chants connect the audience and performers. Brown said in an interview that the style was named Go-Go because "the music just goes and goes." He was known for performances that didn't stop between songs and could go on for several hours.

The park is an open green space that spans one city block and features an inscribed memorial wall at the entrance, where visitors can learn about Brown's impact on the city through a series of photos and timelines. There is also a large play area for young children.

Wind Me Up Chuck, the central sculpture, was created by artist and sculptor Jackie Braitman, who depicts Brown as if he is in motion during a concert. According to her website, the pavilion canopy is 24 feet tall, and the figure of Chuck Brown is 18 feet tall. The total memorial installation is 44 x 28 feet, including the "dance floors," walkway entrances, and landscaping. The installation includes interactive lighting that pulses to the rhythms of Go-Go and responds to visitors' movements.

The Go-Go beat is addictive and makes you want to move your body. It has been sampled by artists from Beyoncé to Jill Scott. The National Symphony Orchestra paid tribute to Brown with two commissioned works and a performance at the US Capitol. His music lives on through the Chuck Brown Band and several others that have been playing Go-Go since Brown created it in the 1970s. Go-Go was designated by DC *Law 23-71* as the Official Music of DC in 2020, and Chuck Brown Day, celebrated annually in various parks around the city in August, is the largest celebration of Go-Go in the nation.

Address 20th & Franklin Streets NE, Washington, DC 20008 | Getting there Bus 83, 86, T14, T18 to Rhode Island Avenue & 18th Street NE | Hours Daily dawn–dusk | Tip Visit HalfSmoke to experience one of DC's favorite halfsmoke sausages – along with a menu packed with tasty treats – and enjoy the Go-Go music playing from the loudspeakers across the street at the iconic Metro PCS store (651 Florida Avenue NW, www.halfsmoke.com).

22 Columbian Harmony Cemetery

A grave injustice

In 1828, a mutual aid society of free Black people established the Harmoneon Cemetery in DC. It filled quickly, and so the graves were moved to the larger Columbian Harmony Cemetery (CHC) site by 1859.

Developer Louis Bell purchased the site in 1960, when the owners fell on hard times. He was to relocate all 37,000 graves to what is now National Harmony Memorial Park in Prince George's County, Maryland. In 2016, however, Virginia State Senator Richard Stuart and his wife Lisa were shocked to discover headstones that were used as riprap to shore up the land along the Potomac River on property they'd purchased. The Stuarts consulted historians, who traced the names to CHC.

An unknown number of graves were not moved, but the headstones were discarded as scrap. While building the Metro station in 1976, workers found at least five coffins and human remains, and city workers digging for a parking lot in 1979 found more remains, pieces of cloth, and coffin fragments, according to an article in *The Washington Post*. Desecration of Black cemeteries for development projects has long been a nationwide issue, beginning in the Jim Crow era.

A plaque at the Rhode Island Avenue-Brentwood Metro Station pays homage to this former resting place of 37,000 African Americans. Among the individuals laid to rest here were Elizabeth Hobbs Keckley, personal dressmaker and confidante of Mary Todd Lincoln; Philip Reid, who helped create the *Statue of Freedom* atop the US Capitol dome; Mary Ann Shad, the first Black female newspaper publisher in North America; Dr. Charles H. Flowers, the main flight instructor of the Tuskegee Airmen during World War II; two sons of abolitionist Frederick Douglass; and countless civilians and Civil War veterans.

Today, efforts continue at CHC to recover and restore the gravestones that once marked the final resting places of so many people.

FORMER SITE
COLUMBIAN HARMONY
CEMETERY
1857-1959

LEST WE FORGET

THIS AREA, INCLUDING THAT OF THE ADJACENT SHOPPING CENTER, WAS ONCE THE SITE OF COLUMBIAN HARMONY CEMETERY. THE CEMETERY, ESTABLISHED IN 1828 "FOR FREE PERSONS OF COLOR," WAS ORIGINALLY LOCATED NEAR 6TH AND S STREETS, NW, WASHINGTON, D.C. RELOCATION OF HARMONY CEMETERY TO THIS AREA BEGAN IN 1857 AND THE CEMETERY WAS ACTIVE HERE ABOUT ONE HUNDRED YEARS. DURING THAT TIME ABOUT 37,000 INTERMENTS OF EMINENT CITIZENS WERE MADE IN THESE ONCE HALLOWED GROUNDS. THIS INCLUDED 531 CIVIL WAR UNION SOLDIERS, WHOSE REMAINS WERE LATER REMOVED TO ARLINGTON NATIONAL CEMETERY, IN VIRGINIA. IN 1959, ALL HUMAN REMAINS IN HARMONY CEMETERY WERE DISINTERRED AND REMOVED TO NATIONAL HARMONY MEMORIAL PARK, IN LARGO, MARYLAND.

THIS MEMORIAL SERVES TO HELP PRESERVE THE MEMORY OF THE HISTORICALLY IMPORTANT HARMONY CEMETERY SITE AND TO HONOR THE LOVED ONES ONCE INTERRED HERE.

Address 919 Rhode Island Avenue NE, Washington, DC 20018, www.humanitiestruck.com/what-lies-beneath | Getting there Metro to Rhode Island Avenue-Brentwood (Red Line); bus P6, D8, H8, H9, S41, T14, T18 to Rhode Island Avenue-Brentwood | Hours Unrestricted | Tip The internationally acclaimed artist Lois Mailou Jones lived on Quincy Street from the 1950s until the 1970s. Her work can be viewed at the Smithsonian's American Art Museum, the Metropolitan Museum of Art, the National Museum of Women in the Arts and many others (1220 Quincy Street NE).

23 Congressional Cemetery

A veritable who's who in DC history

A walk through Congressional Cemetery is like traveling through more than 200 years of history. The cemetery is beautifully land-scaped, and it's hard to believe that it was once neglected. By the 1980s, stones had crumbled, and the grass grew tall.

The cemetery, owned by Christ Church, was formally established in 1807. The website notes that 100 burial sites were set aside in 1820 for the interment of members of Congress. With additional sites donated to or purchased by the government, it came to be known as Congressional Cemetery. Laid out in rectangular sections, it's easy to navigate, and you'll find many notable figures among almost 70,000 people buried here.

The cemetery comes to life through events and guided tours by trained docents between April and October on Saturdays and occasional Sundays, online reservations required. Past tours and events have included a Sunday Stroll guided tour of the cemetery; a poetry open mic night for open dialogues about life, death, and the in-between; chamber concerts; and a speaker's series focusing on selected graves. A few of the final resting places you will visit on the cemetery's Introductory Tour are that of composer John Philip Sousa, designer of the US Capitol building Dr. William Thornton, former DC Mayor Marion Barry, and Choctaw Indian Chief Push-Ma-Ta-Ha, who fought during the War of 1812 and was buried with full military honors.

You can download maps from the website for at least 20 themed, self-guided, walking tours. Wander through the cemetery following themed routes that include African Americans, American Indians, the LGBTQIA+ community, and civil rights leaders. Two notable figures interred here are Alain Leroy Locke, who was the first Black Rhodes Scholar and is also considered the first gay person to hold that honor, and Tyrone Gayle, who served as the Washington press secretary for then-Senator Kamala Harris.

Address 1801 E Street SE, Washington, DC 20003, +1 (202) 543-0539, www.congressionalcemetery.org, staff@congressionalcemetery.org | Getting there Metro to Potomac Avenue (Blue, Orange, Silver Lines); bus B2 to Potomac Avenue & 18th Street SE | Hours Daily dawn–dusk | Tip The Anacostia Arts Center is a community space featuring small, Black-owned businesses. Check out an original play or performance at the Black Box Theater and browse the shops (1231 Good Hope Road SE, www.anacostiaartscenter.com).

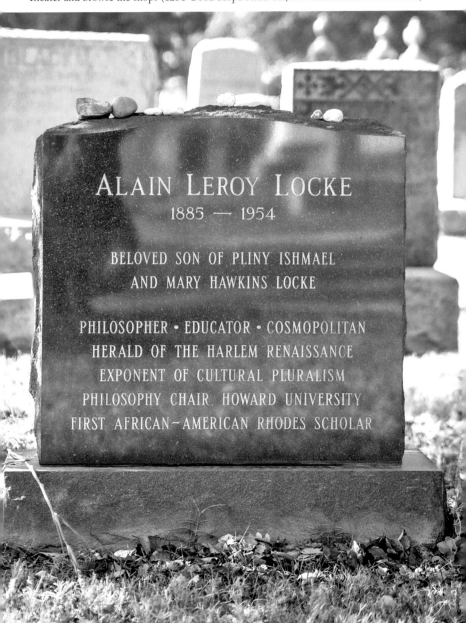

24 CYCLED!
Your new happy place for fitness

CYCLED! is a boutique studio that offers members fitness options through a combination of yoga, barre, strength, and indoor cycling classes. The staff members provide unforgettable workout experiences for people who want to try something new or switch up their fitness routines. Owner and Chief Happiness Officer Dr. Shayla Cornick wants members to enjoy their workouts by engaging in classes at the level that's right for them. "I love helping people feel good about themselves," says Dr. Cornick.

The entrance to CYCLED! is bright and decorated with greenery and orchids. The stylish cycle studio, on the ground floor just behind the welcome desk, is where you'll hop on a bike for a spin class that's guaranteed to make you sweat. A white neon sign against a black wall reads, "CYCLED! is my Happy Place." Dr. Cornick and team bring the energy to every class with a mix of urban music that sets the pace for a serious cardio workout.

CYCLED! has built up a diverse membership of people from the community, and there are even members who travel from as far as Baltimore to participate in classes. Dr. Cornick started her studio while working in educational research, which involved a great deal of travel. She enjoyed taking classes at a variety of cycling studios while on the road, but she noticed that instructors never looked like her, or they didn't often play the type of urban and popular music she enjoys. "I wanted to create something for people like me who wanted something different in terms of the music," says Dr. Cornick. "And I also wanted to showcase something different in terms of what a cycling instructor looks like."

The loft level upstairs contains space for yoga, barre, and strength classes. The towels are free, water is available for purchase, and classes are offered seven days a week. Everyone is welcome to become a part of the CYCLED! community.

Address 6960 C Maple Street NW, Washington, DC 20012, +1 (240) 641-4969, www.cycledstudios.com, info@CYCLEDstudios.com | Getting there Metro to Takoma (Red Line); bus 12, 13, 16, 18, 25 to Carroll & Maple Avenues NW | Hours Check website for schedule | Tip Nearby Busboys and Poets is a restaurant, bar, bookstore, and community gathering place with eight locations in the area. The name refers to poet Langston Hughes, who worked as a busboy at the Wardman Park Hotel in the 1920s (235 Carroll Street NW, www.busboysandpoets.com).

25 DCity Smokehouse
DC-style BBQ

BBQ lovers know that enjoying the smoky flavors is often an experience best shared with family and friends, and it goes beyond the food. Melvin Hines, founder of Southeast Restaurant Group, understands barbecue and makes it easy for you to have that delicious experience without having to fire up your own smoker.

Hines founded DCity Smokehouse in 2013, giving DC BBQ its own distinctive style. "My main focus is consistency and wanting you to have the same experience, whether it's today, next week or next year, and the team works to maintain that from day to day in the restaurant," says Hines. "There is a distinct taste profile between a little bit of spice and a little bit of sweet that's intentional."

The menu includes smoked meats and poultry, sandwiches, and sides. Specialties include their bestselling smoked chicken wings and popular Meaty Palmer, a sandwich made with turkey breast, pork belly, avocado, tomato, and chipotle aioli. According to Hines, "The BBQ concept is all about time – 18 hours for the brisket, 6 hours for the wings. Low and slow is what we believe in." Hines sees customers from South America, Asia, and different parts of the world, in addition to regular customers, who may stop by a couple of times a week. The joy for Hines is in watching people from diverse backgrounds enjoy the food.

The words WE SMOKE MEATS are emblazoned in red on the side of the patio, and a red pig statue welcomes all customers. You'd never know that you're dining in a former 1940s television repair shop. Hines transformed it into a hub for community connections and great food. The space feels like a place that you want to sit a while, with big-screen TVs, an indoor/outdoor patio with red-covered picnic tables and benches, and indoor dining tables next to a full-service bar. A wall contains the menu, which is surrounded by posters and information related to local Black culture.

Address 203 Florida Avenue NW, Washington, DC 20001, +1 (202) 733-1919, www.dcitysmokehouse.com, dcitysmokehouse@gmail.com | Getting there Metro to Shaw (Green Line); bus 90, 92 to Florida Avenue & 2nd Street NW | Hours Sun–Thu 11am–11pm, Fri & Sat 11am–midnight | Tip Less than a mile away is a set of street pole banners marking various events that took place in the NoMa neighborhood, including several at the former Uline Arena. Look for the banner featuring Earl Lloyd, the first Black athlete to play in an NBA game in 1950 (3rd Street NE, south side of M Street).

26   Decatur House

A little known story of bravery

The Decatur House was built between 1818 and 1819 by Navy war hero Stephen Decatur, Jr. (1779–1820), who built the home with the money he received for his efforts in the War of 1812. It was the first residential structure in the neighborhood of the White House. Today, the house helps to preserve the story of the United States, which includes the involuntary enslavement of African Americans.

Decatur lived in this grand, three-story Federal-style brick townhome with his wife Susan. Benjamin Henry Latrobe, the first professional American architect and engineer, designed it with ample space for entertaining. But they enjoyed their home for only 14 months. Decatur died here as the result of an ultimately fatal gunshot wound he suffered in a duel held in Bladensburg, Maryland on the morning of March 22, 1820.

Decatur House includes the last known standing enslaved quarters in an urban area. One of the enslaved people at Decatur House was Charlotte Dupuy, who famously and bravely sued her enslaver Secretary of State Henry Clay for her freedom. She contended that she was entitled to her freedom because her mother and grandmother were both free, along with the assurance of freedom from her former enslaver. Clay was instructed by the court to leave Dupuy behind when he moved back to his Kentucky home, and so he took her husband and children with him. Dupuy continued to live in Decatur House, now assumed by the home's next resident, Secretary of State Martin Van Buren. The court ultimately ruled against Dupuy, and she was forcibly taken to the New Orleans residence of Clay's daughter. In 1840, 11 years after the lawsuit, Clay freed Dupuy and her daughter Mary Ann. Four years later, he freed her son Charles.

A free tour allows you to view several areas of the house, including the restored Slave Quarters, approximately 900 square feet, where up to 21 people were housed.

Address 1610 H Street NW, Washington, DC 20006, +1 (202) 218-4333, www.whitehousehistory.org, customerservice@whha.org | Getting there Metro to Farragut West (Blue, Orange, Silver Lines); bus 11Y, 32, 33, 36, 80, X2 to H & 17th Streets NW | Hours Mon–Fri 9am–5pm; book online for free tours Mon 10:30am & 1pm | Tip Look for the callbox marker in honor of Elizabeth Hobbs Keckley (1818–1907), dressmaker and confidante to First Lady Mary Todd Lincoln. Born into slavery in Virginia, Keckley would help found organizations to assist formerly enslaved people and later taught at Wilberforce University in Ohio (1432 K Street NW).

27 Department of the Interior

A hidden haven for art lovers

From the outside, the Department of the Interior's Stewart Lee Udall Building, named after the agency's 37th secretary, looks no different than other nearby agencies. Completed in 1936, the seven-story, steel-framed structure is clad in granite and limestone. It was designed and built under President Franklin D. Roosevelt's New Deal, which was a series of programs and projects instituted during the Great Depression with the aim of restoring prosperity to Americans. But it's what's inside this building that is practically unknown to many Washingtonians.

The 32nd Secretary of the Interior Harold Ickes (1874–1952) was closely involved in the construction of the building. It includes more than 2,200 offices, each exposed to natural light due to five interior courtyards. Ickes ensured that modern conveniences were available for the staff, such as a gymnasium, a cafeteria, a library, and the first central air conditioning installed in a federal building. A museum and a wonderful Native American arts and crafts shop are open to the public.

Ickes was a great proponent of the arts and personally managed the installation of over 40 murals created by New Deal-era artists that you can see on guided tours. Look for the vibrant scenes of Black contributions to science, art, education, and religion by artist Millard Owen Sheets (1907–1989), and 26 photomurals of iconic natural and man-made sites by Ansel Adams (1902–1984).

After the tour, walk to the courtyard adjacent to the cafeteria to find *Negro Mother and Child,* a six-foot-tall, bronze casting by Maurice Glickman (1906–1961). It was seen by thousands at the 1939 New York World's Fair before its permanent installation at this out-of-the-way site. The beautiful statue shows a mother with her arms crossed and eyes fixed forward. She is relaxed and confident but also guarded and reserved. Her son stands close to her.

Address 1849 C Street NW, Washington, DC 20240, +1 (202) 208-4743, www.doi.gov/
interiormuseum/plan-a-visit | Getting there Metro to Farragut West (Blue, Orange, Silver Lines)
or Farragut North (Red Line); bus 16Y, 3Y to 19th Street & Virginia Avenue NW; DC Circu-
lator to Constitution Avenue & 18th Street NW (National Mall Line) | Hours Mon–Fri
9am–5pm, Tours Tue & Thu 2pm | Tip The Octagon Museum is DC's oldest residence, built
for an extremely wealthy planter in 1799. The ongoing exhibit, "I Was Here," commemorates
the lives of the enslaved people who built and worked there (1799 New York Avenue NW,
www.architectsfoundation.org/octagon-museum).

28 Duke Ellington Memorial
Celebrating a native son

One of the greatest musicians of all time was born and raised in Washington, DC. The son of two pianists, Edward "Duke" Kennedy Ellington (1899–1974) likely had music in his genes. His style, grace, and good manners made him seem like royalty, hence the nickname "The Duke." He started taking piano lessons at the age of seven and composed his first musical number "Soda Fountain Rag" at the age of 14, while working after school at the Poodle Dog Café, which was on Georgia Avenue NW. He left home for New York City in 1923 near the beginning of the Harlem Renaissance, and by the mid-1920s, he was an established band leader with his own orchestra playing at the famous Cotton Club.

The Duke Ellington Memorial *Encore* is a stainless steel and granite statue, by Zachary Oxman, that features Ellington seated in an outsized treble clef and playing a curved piano. Duke is giving a cue to an orchestra as if in a frozen moment in time. You can almost hear "Take the A Train" in the background. Ellington was successful largely due to his ability to keep his sound fresh throughout the changing times.

Ellington often visited DC and performed at dozens of local clubs and theaters along the U Street corridor, which was known as Black Broadway. The city was segregated until the 1950s, but Black people could and did own more than 200 businesses, making this area economically and culturally rich. Ellington was among the very first Black musicians to celebrate his race and proudly use the word "Black" in many of his song titles, rather than stick to stereotypes or play it safe.

Ellington's father worked at several jobs for a prominent local doctor and then part-time as a butler in the White House in the early 1920s. His parents would have been proud to attend their son's 70th birthday in 1969, celebrated by a historic reception and jam session and hosted by President Nixon at the White House.

Address Florida Avenue & T Street NW, Washington, DC 20001 | Getting there Metro to Shaw-Howard University (Green Line); bus 90, 92 to Florida & Georgia Avenues NW | Hours Unrestricted | Tip The Howard Theater was built in 1910 and was the largest theater for Black audiences, long before the famous Apollo Theater in Harlem. Over the course of its first 70 years, just about every top Black entertainer in the United States performed on its stage (620 T Street NW, www.thehowardtheatre.com).

Eaton DC – Allegory

A new look at Alice in Wonderland

Eaton DC is a boutique hotel focused on community, creativity, and culture, described as "a welcoming and inclusive cultural hub for kindred spirits, locals, and travelers alike, to convene, collaborate, and create." Indeed, there is much to discover and experience at this one-of-a-kind hotel, including cultural programming, wellness workshops, and rooftop parties, which often feature local talent.

Stop in to view the art on display throughout the hotel. Former First Lady Michelle Obama is reported to have visited to take a look. According to curator Sheldon Scott, "Eaton's curatorial focus is on artists that reflect our local and global perspective and speak to intersecting environmental and social issues. This is a platform for some of the best, brightest, and most promising artists in the Washington, DC area aligned with Eaton's philosophy."

And hidden behind a nondescript door is one of the features here at Eaton that you must not miss: Allegory, the hotel speakeasy.

Lewis Carroll's *Alice in Wonderland* and *Through the Looking Glass* stories have taken over the dimly lit space with a whimsical design featuring a black bar, bar stools, and lounge furniture. The allegory in this room is depicted in a fantastic mural by artist Erik Thor Sandberg, who has reimagined the classic Carroll stories told not through the eyes of Alice, but of Ruby Bridges, the first Black child to desegregate the William Frantz Elementary School in Louisiana in 1960. Bridges is now a well-known civil rights activist and author, and she is founder of the Ruby Bridges Foundation, dedicated to offering programs and resources that empower youth to end racism and all forms of discrimination and create more harmony throughout the world.

Allegory is loved by locals and travelers for its top-notch service and whimsical and imaginative drink creations, which continue to reflect the allegory in the design.

1201 K Street NW, Washington, DC 20005, +1 (202) 289-7600, www.allegory-dc.com
Metro to McPherson Square (Blue, Orange, Silver Lines); bus D4 to 13th &
K Streets NW, or bus 63, 64, G8 to 11th & K Streets NW; DC Circulator to 13th & K Streets NW
(Georgetown-Union Station Line)   Mon–Thu 5pm–midnight, Fri & Sat 5pm–2am

Mr. Braxton Bar & Kitchen is an American Bistro featuring great food, drinks, live music, and touches of an *Alice in Wonderland* vibe on their cool patio (3632 Georgia Avenue NW, www.mrbraxton.com).

30 Eighth+Kin
Brown girl approved

Finding the right makeup and skincare products can be challenging, particularly for women of color. Retail establishments carry only a small percentage of products from Black beauty brands, and they're often found in one aisle dedicated to "ethnic" products. These products rarely work for the many skin tones and hair types embodied by women of color, who are always hunting for products that work. "Black consumers are three times more likely to be dissatisfied than non-Black consumers with their options for hair care, skin care, and makeup," according to a 2022 report by global management consulting firm McKinsey & Company.

Enter Kimberly Smith, founder of Eighth+Kin, a bright and welcoming retail space just south of Dupont Circle. Smith, an attorney, launched her business in 2017 as the first online beauty retailer to curate products exclusively from beauty brands by owners who are Black, Indigenous, and People of Color (BIPOC). "We feature prestige brands that elevate the natural beauty in all skin tones," says Smith.

Customers can choose from a range of products, including a line from Smith's own in-house collection Amanzi Skin, or a popular UK-based brand Trepadora for naturally curly hair. In-person services include bridal consultations; "The Bombshell" glam sessions to provide you with the perfect look for a special occasion, date night, or the office; and "Teach Me How To Do It" lessons to teach you how to apply your own makeup.

Growing up, Smith always had a passion for fashion and beauty, and she was inspired by her grandmother, whom she describes as the first fashionista she ever met. Her grandmother defied the norms and expressed her sense of fashion with bright and bold colors, along with a collection of wigs and stylish jewelry. "Expressing myself through different hairstyles, make-up, and fashion, has always been fun for me," says Smith.

1365 Connecticut Avenue NW, Suite 100, Washington, DC 20036, +1 (202) 506-2582, www.eighthandkin.com, experience@eighthandkin.com   Metro to Dupont Circle (Red Line); bus 42, N2, N4, N6 to Connecticut Avenue & Dupont Circle NW; DC Circulator to 19th & N Streets NW (Dupont Circle-Rosslyn Line)   Wed–Sat noon–6pm, Sun noon–4pm   Skin Beauty Bar on Capitol Hill offers a wide range of services by highly trained therapists, including tanning, eyebrow/lash tint, eyelash lift, and body contouring (749 8th Street SE, 2nd Floor, www.skinbeautybardc.com).

31 Elements Urban Arts Collective

The power of dance and dreams

Energy and creativity are in overdrive at Elements Urban Arts Collective (EUAC). If you have children who love Hip Hop and urban dance, you'll want to enroll them in classes here. The dancing and music are so contagious that you might find yourself signing up for an adult class to join in the fun!

Alana Hill is the founder and director of EUAC. She has been an arts educator and administrator for 16 years, serving the DC local arts community in the areas of dance and theater. "I started EUAC in 2017 to honor and elevate Hip Hop and Urban Arts," she shares. "Many years ago, I found myself on the outs of a ballet studio when it was revealed to me that I didn't have the body or aesthetic for ballet. I was a young child at the time, but those words echoed throughout my life as I struggled to be taken seriously as a dancer without having the privilege of a ballet background."

Hill is fulfilling her dreams and those of the many young dancers who come through her doors. She provides instruction for all ages, from Hip Hop FUN-Damentals for grades K–2 to Jazz Technique and Choreography, or Hip Hop Technique and Choreography for grades 3–12. Summer camps are also available for ages 5–13. EUAC's offerings also include the Elements Dance Company, a pre-professional Urban Dance training program for dancers ages 8 – 18, who receive education in all forms of Urban Dance, such as b-boying/b-girling, Hip Hop, locking, popping, house, krumping, waacking, voguing, and various forms of commercial dance. Dancers also have an opportunity to train with industry professionals and perform at many noteworthy events and venues.

"It's time for us to redefine what makes art great," Hill says, "and to ensure that all young artists feel that who they are and how they look can never limit what they can be!"

Address 12015 Nebel Street, North Bethesda, MD 20852, +1 (240) 339-3822, www.elementsuac.com, info@elementsuac.com | Getting there Metro to North Bethesda (Red Line) | Hours Mon, Wed–Fri 5–9pm, Sat & Sun 8:30am–1pm | Tip Nearby Urban Artistry, Inc. is an internationally recognized non-profit organization dedicated to the performance and preservation of art forms inspired by the urban experience. Urban Artistry focuses on urban dance forms born in Black and Brown urban communities (11308 Grandview Avenue, Silver Spring, MD, www.urbanartistry.org).

32 Emancipation Memorial
A controversial tribute

On the morning after Abraham Lincoln's death in 1865, formerly enslaved Charlotte Scott donated five dollars to her employer and asked that it be used towards a monument to the president's memory. A campaign among free Black Americans raised $18,000, the equivalent of almost $350,000 today, for such a memorial.

Frederick Douglass delivered the keynote speech at the dedication of the Emancipation Memorial on April 14, 1876. President Ulysses S. Grant and other dignitaries were also in attendance. The statue served as the primary national memorial for Lincoln until 1922, when the Lincoln Memorial was dedicated on the National Mall.

The Emancipation Memorial depicts a life-sized figure of Abraham Lincoln extending one hand over a kneeling Black man while holding a copy of the Emancipation Proclamation in the other hand. His wrist shackles broken, the Black man appears to be rising. The figure was modeled after Archer Alexander, the last enslaved man captured under the Fugitive Slave Law.

However, no Black people were asked to share ideas for the memorial. Douglass later wrote a letter to a local newspaper criticizing the statue's design. "The Negro here, though rising, is still on his knees and nude," Douglass wrote. "What I want to see before I die is a monument representing the Negro, not couchant on his knees like a four-footed animal, but erect on his feet like a man."

The police killing of George Floyd in 2020 reignited efforts across the US to take down statues viewed as symbols of slavery and racism. Fierce arguments broke out about the Emancipation Memorial. Some felt that the statue was demeaning and ignored the pivotal role enslaved people played in gaining their own freedom. The other side pointed out that the statue was funded by formerly enslaved people and didn't want to erase this history. The fate of the memorial remains to be seen.

Address Lincoln Park Drive NE, Washington, DC 20002, www.nps.gov/places/000/
emancipation-memorial.htm | Getting there Metro to Eastern Market (Blue, Orange, Silver
Lines), transfer to bus 90 or 96 to 8th & East Capitol Street NE | Hours Daily dawn–dusk |
Tip A plaque on the Enlightened building commemorates Freedom's Crossing, a way across
the Anacostia River taken by countless Black people fleeing slavery in Maryland towards
freedom in the District of Columbia as a result of the Compensated Emancipation Act
(1205 Good Hope Road SE, www.adaciancestors.org).

33 Engine Company No. 4 Building

Honoring those who chose to serve

The building looks like a fire station, but it's actually a townhouse with an interesting history. Built in 1885, it once housed the first fire company in DC with only Black firefighters. The building was renovated in 2017, keeping the beautiful façade intact. The No. 7 painted at the top references Company No. 7, the first to inhabit this building. After consolidating, the Fire Department moved the all-Black Engine Company No. 4 from Southwest DC to this location in Northwest.

The DC Fire Department had employed a few Black firefighters after it professionalized in the 1870s, but none had ever achieved officer status. In 1918, 16-year veteran Private Charles E. Gibson, Private Frank Hall, and Private Richard J. Holmes proposed the idea of a separate unit, and the Fire Department agreed. Engine Company No. 4 was established April 3, 1919.

The Sep 27, 1941, issue of the Afro-American newspaper featured Engine Company No. 4 at their one-year anniversary party commemorating their move into the R Street location. They reported that the company had set a record by answering 750 alarms in one year. The paper stated "the company is said to have one of the best records in the DC Fire Department. Virtually all of its members won commendations from the public and municipal officials during the Knickerbocker Theater disaster of 1922". The Knickerbocker disaster was one of the most devastating tragedies in DC when the Adams Morgan theater's roof collapsed during a movie due to a heavy snowfall, killing 98 and injuring another 133.

In 1943 the famous African American photographer Gordon Parks documented Engine Company No. 4 in a series of photographs that can be viewed at the Library of Congress. The marker on the front of the building includes one of Parks' photos.

Address 931 R Street NW, Washington, DC 20001 | Getting there Metro to Shaw-Howard U (Green, Yellow Lines); bus 70 to 7th & R Streets NW | Hours Unrestricted from the outside only | Tip Doro Soul food is the inspiration of Michelin-starred chef Elias Taddesse, who combines traditional American soul food with Ethiopian flavors. Try buttermilk-marinated chicken naked (mild), berbere (hot) or mitmita (very hot). Carry out only (1819 7th Street NW, www.dorosoulfood.com).

34 Everyday Sundae
Next level chef

Charles Foreman, a classically trained chef who worked for establishments such as the Four Seasons and The Palm, had to decide how to move forward for himself and his family when unemployment struck because of the pandemic. The mouthwatering result is Everyday Sundae, a premium ice cream shop serving the Petworth community with delightful frozen treats.

Consider flavors such as Perfect Peaches & Cream with real peach slices; "Warm Hug Banana Pudding" with banana ice cream, marshmallows and vanilla wafers; and "Divine Bourbon Truffle" with brown butter ice cream, salted caramel, and buttery bourbon truffles. However, don't get your heart set on finding any one flavor any time you stop by. Foreman rotates the menu daily from his collection of 52 recipes. And do not miss Warm Waffle Wednesdays, when Foreman selects a different flavor of ice cream and waffle to feature and presents this delicious concoction complete with a chef-inspired garnish.

Foreman has lived here in Petworth for more than 20 years and has seen all types of people come and go as the area has been going through gentrification. His aim was to provide a sweet spot in the community where everyone is welcome. Foreman lives his life based on a principle that he learned in his college fraternity Omega Psi Phi, "It's not what you have but what you give." He keeps a "Scoop Fund" to provide free ice cream for kids who can't afford it and has many stories of people contributing to the fund to help pay this kindness forward. In addition, he regularly reads children's books to a group of local school children, complete with free ice cream.

The community expresses their appreciation for Foreman by writing letters, which he posts on the "Love Wall" inside of the shop. When you visit, you can expect to feel the love of great ice cream, fantastic service, and an owner that cares about his community.

Address 713 Kennedy Street NW, Washington, DC 20011, +1 (202) 723-0159, www.everydaysundaedc.com, hello@everydaysundaeDC.com | Getting there Metro to Fort Totten (Red Line), then transfer to bus E4 to 7th & Kennedy Streets NW | Hours Wed–Sun 3–9pm | Tip Owner Paulos Belay brings his authentic, hometown, Detroit-style pizza to DC at the Motown Square Pizza carryout. Fans of the hit 90s TV series *Martin* will want to order the "Jerome's in the House" pizza with Wisconsin brick cheese, mozzarella, pepperoni, bell peppers, mushrooms and crushed tomatoes (1819 7th Street NW, www.motownsquaredc.com).

35 The Extra Mile
Americans as forces for change

The Extra Mile-Points of Light Volunteer Pathway honors the actions and service of 34 Americans who have transformed the nation and the world. There is a bas-relief of each honoree on 42-inch, bronze medallions set into the sidewalk.

Two of the honorees are W. E. B. Du Bois and Booker T. Washington. They were leaders in the 19th and early 20th centuries who both wanted social and economic equality for Black people but disagreed on how to achieve their goals.

Du Bois (1868 – 1963) was born a free man in Massachusetts. He attended Fisk University and then Harvard, where he became the first African American to receive a PhD in 1895. Du Bois espoused the concept of the "Talented Tenth," emphasizing the necessity for higher education to develop the leadership capacity among the most able 10 percent of Black Americans to achieve political and civil equality. He feared that the overemphasis on industrial training would confine Black people permanently to the ranks of second-class citizenship. Du Bois co-founded the National Association for the Advancement of Colored People (NAACP).

Washington (1856 – 1915) was born into slavery in Virginia. His father was a white man, and his mother was an African woman. Washington attended Hampton University and became an educator, reformer, and the most influential Black leader of his time. He believed in self-help and urged Black people to tolerate discrimination for the time being and concentrate on elevating themselves through hard work and material prosperity. He supported education in the crafts, industries, and farming skills to win the respect of whites and acceptance as fully integrated citizens.

Stroll along the path to encounter change makers, including investigative journalist Ida B. Wells-Barnett, Civil Rights Leader Dorothy Height, and Clara Barton, Founder of the American Red Cross.

THE EXTRA MILE

Points of Light Volunteer Pathway

IN 1909, W.E.B. DUBOIS, A LEADING SPOKESMAN IN THE CAMPAIGN FOR RACIAL EQUALITY, JOINED MARY WHITE OVINGTON, MOORFIELD STOREY, WILLIAM ENGLISH WALLING, JOHN MILHOLLAND, OSWALD GARRISON VILLARD, FRANCES BLASCOER AND 54 OTHER PROMINENT AMERICANS AS FOUNDING OFFICERS OF THE NAACP. BOTH OVINGTON AND DUBOIS SERVED IN CRUCIAL ROLES AT THE NAACP FOR DECADES, HELPING GUIDE ITS POLICIES AND PROGRAMS.

believe that all men, ck and brown and white, brothers, varying in time opportunity, in form gift and feature, but ring in no essential icular, and alike in soul the possibility of ite development."
W.E.B. DUBOIS

W.E.B. DuBois 1868–1963

Mary White Ovington 1865–195

Pennsylvania Avenue & 15th Street NW, Washington, DC 20004
Metro to McPherson Square (Blue, Orange, Silver Lines); bus 11Y, 32, 36 to 15th Street &
New York Avenue NW   Unrestricted   Every US President has either visited or
stayed at the Willard Hotel since the 1850s, and Dr. Martin Luther King, Jr. prepared for his
"I Have a Dream" speech in his room here. Indulge yourself in afternoon tea, and be sure to
view their history gallery (1401 Pennsylvania Avenue, www.washington.intercontinental.com).

36 Fia's Fabulous Finds
Modern day treasure hunting

"Owning a second-hand boutique is not just my dream job, but a lifestyle," says Safisha "Fia" Thomas, owner of Fia's Fabulous Finds. Fia and her husband Frank have owned their boutique for almost a decade. Thomas continues, "I started this business because I love a good bargain and quality items at fabulous prices."

If you love bargains too, don't miss a chance to open the shop's pink door and browse through the racks. When you walk in, you'll see pictures of Black women pioneers from Pam Grier to Josephine Baker adorning the walls, and Fia's bright smile welcomes you. She will help guide you through two small rooms packed with merchandise and help you find something you can't live without. Thomas sources her goods from community consignments and shopping closeouts from major retailers. She primarily carries gently used clothing for women from a variety of brands, casual to upscale, in sizes 0-4X. Brands have included Marine Layer, Patagonia, Vintage, Ralph Lauren, and Neiman Marcus. You can also find jewelry and accessories, children's clothing, men's accessories, and unique household items, like retro styles of dishware and fun household signs.

Thomas' inventory changes frequently. Once you are connected with the shop via social media, you'll find out about their exciting live sales in which Thomas quickly goes through a large portion of inventory in an auction style format, and customers place bids for items. She also hosts in-person events when you get to "fill a bag" for a very reasonable flat fee.

Thomas is proud of her heritage and describes herself as a Black woman continually striving for success, while staying true to herself and her community. She further states, "My goal is to support any woman, specifically Black and brown women, who wish to open businesses, and I have created an incubator for many, allowing them to sell their items in my boutique."

Address 806 Upshur Street NW, Washington, DC 20011, +1 (202) 492-8278,
www.fiasfabulousfinds.com, info@fiasfabulousfinds.com | **Getting there** Metro to Georgia
Avenue-Petworth (Green Line); bus 60 to Upshur & 9th Streets NW | **Hours** Tue–Sat
noon–7pm, Sun noon–6pm, Mon by appointment | **Tip** Bespoke Not Broke is a unique
boutique in MD that specializes in vintage, consignment, and upscale resale clothing
and accessories for men, women, and children (7042 Carroll Avenue, Takoma Park, MD,
bespokenotbroke.com).

37 FishScale

Best of the Bay

The fish fry is a tradition at many Black family cookouts, especially during the summer months. The Northwest eatery FishScale cooks up a delicious and healthy re-interpretation of the fish fry that diners can enjoy all year round. The day-to-day operations of the organic farm-to-table and ocean-to-table restaurant are managed by co-owners Henry Brandon Williams, the executive chef, and his sister Kristal Williams, the director of operations.

Henry prepared his first-ever fish burger on the grill at a cookout. His mother had adopted a pescatarian lifestyle, and he wanted to ensure that she had something to eat amongst all the meat and poultry dishes on the menu. The fish burgers were such a hit, the story goes, that his mother had a hard time even getting her hands on one! Today, FishScale serves an all-fish burger, and they don't add breadcrumbs or any other fillers.

The signature dishes here have an international flare, with American, Asian, and Caribbean flavors coming into play throughout the menu. The offerings include crab burgers, cheesesteaks, chef's plates, and a version of fish n' chips. You can order special accompaniments, including Japanese sweet potatoes, vegetarian collards, and sunflower yogurt coleslaw.

According to Chef Williams, "We source from local organic farmers and retailers, and source seafood, according to the Monterey Bay Seafood Watch standards, from local and US fishermen." He is devoted to promoting human health and earth sustainability.

FishScale first debuted at the White House Farmer's Market, and their current location in the Shaw neighborhood opened in 2017. The restaurant is great for carry-out and also has a small seating area if you prefer to dine in. FishScale also plays a role in their neighborhood, providing employment for underserved communities and partnering with several non-profit and student organizations.

Address 637 Florida Avenue NW, Washington, DC 20001, +1 (202) 780-7886, www.wearefishscale.com | Getting there Metro to Shaw-Howard U (Green Line); bus 90, 92, 96 to Florida Georgia Avenues NW | Hours Wed & Thu 11:30am–7pm, Fri & Sat 11:30am–8pm | Tip Horace & Dickies seafood carryout is a beloved DC institution. They were on H Street for more than 30 years, but you can now find their famous fried seafood and side dishes at their newest location in Takoma Park, DC (6912 4th Street NW, www.horaceanddickies.com).

38 Flora Moulton Call Box

Spreading the Gospel for more than 40 years

Hidden in plain sight on the streets of DC are some historic artifacts that have been given new life. Call boxes were installed following the Civil War, thus pre-dating radio communications and the 911 system. By 1891, all police precincts contained patrol call boxes and dozens of fire alarm call boxes. These devices were vital tools for emergency communication. A citizen could summon the fire department, or a beat cop could report into the precinct house. Today, many of the remaining call boxes have been restored through a city-wide effort led by Cultural Tourism DC or other neighborhood organizations.

Flora Rollins Molton (1908–1990) was an American gospel and blues artist who described her music as "spiritual and truth music." A native of Louisa County, Virginia and the daughter of a Baptist minister, she arrived in the District in 1937, joining her brother Rev. Robert L. Rollins, who was a minister at the Florida Avenue Baptist Church. She began singing in the street in the 1940s to supplement her income. She played slide guitar, a technique common to many rural blues artists. She simultaneously tapped a tambourine with her foot and later added a harmonica.

Molton was born with a visual impairment that left her legally blind, but this disability did not hinder her from pursuing a calling to share her spirituality. She could be found performing regularly at 7th and F Streets NW and later at 11th and F.

Her legacy helps tell the story of a generation of Southern Black migrants, who brought a rich tradition of African American and gospel music north. She won four awards for artistic excellence from the DC Commission on Arts and Humanities. During her lifetime, she sang at the Smithsonian Institution's Festival of American Folklife on the National Mall, at the Library of Congress, and at the former Capital Center with the Rolling Stones.

Address 13th & G Streets NW, Washington, DC 20005, +1 (202) 783-5144, historicsites.dcpreservation.org, info@dcpreservation.org | **Getting there** Metro to Metro Center (Blue, Orange, Red, Silver Lines); bus D6 to 13th & G Streets NW | **Hours** Unrestricted | **Tip** Take the free, self-guided tour at The Sumner School, named for Charles Sumner, Massachusetts Senator, ardent abolitionist. The oldest Black public school building still extant, it has remained substantially unaltered both inside and out and now houses a museum and archives for DC public school records and artifacts (1201 17th Street NW, www.sumnerschoolmuseum.org).

39 Flowers by Alexes
Continuing a family legacy

Imagine a childhood filled with flowers. That's how Alexes Haggins grew up in her father's flower shop on the same street where they lived in Petworth. Bernard Haggins was a beloved fixture in the neighborhood. In the early 1960s, he worked as a delivery driver for a local florist and took over the business when the owner retired. He met Alexes' mother Edwina when she was working for Industrial Bank nearby.

Bernard changed the business' name to "Flowers by Alexes" to honor the birth of his daughter. Alexes started working in the shop when she was old enough, assisting with sales and making deliveries. Bernard operated the shop for more than 40 years until he passed in 2004, and the shop closed.

But in 2022, Alexes reopened the shop in a corner building with a welcoming entrance. You'll find beautiful and colorful cut flowers and plants for sale and order custom arrangements. Alexes once received a request for an arrangement made with proteas, the robust, exotic flower that's chiefly native to South Africa, to match the customer's wallpaper. You might find Alexes instructing a group of customers on how to select fresh cut flowers and then arranging the flowers for presentation as gifts. She tells them how to extend their flowers' lives by cutting the stems before arranging them in a vase. It is easy to see that she loves what she does. Her daughter Willo may be following in her footsteps – she loves helping her mom and is also very creative. Haggins' plans for the shop include adding more instructional classes, increasing the shop's offerings and expanding to a second location.

She stays grounded by disconnecting from her phone on her days off, occasionally staying in bed all day, going to the spa or just having mommy time with her four children. "Taking care of my health is important to make sure I don't burn out mentally or physically," she says.

Address 851 Upshur Street NW, Washington, DC 20011, +1 (202) 910-7490, www.flowersbyalexes.com | **Getting there** Metro to Georgia Avenue-Petworth (Green Line), then walk 9 minutes; bus 60, 62, 63, 70, 78 to Georgia Avenue & Upshur Street NW | **Hours** Tue – Fri 9am – 5:30pm, Sat 9am – 1pm | **Tip** (*Here I stand*) *In the Spirit of Paul Robeson* is a nearby sculpture by Allen Uzikee Nelson that honors the legacy of the actor, singer, lawyer, athlete, and activist (917 Varnum Street, NW).

40 Fort Reno Park

Curiouser and curiouser

Fort Reno Park sits at 429 feet above sea level, the highest elevation in the city. The Union Army used this advantage to construct one of the most heavily armed fortifications during the Civil War. Once the war was over, Fort Reno was abandoned and became a reservoir station with an accompanying sandstone castle, which you can still see towering above the park.

Today, the park continues a tradition that began in the 1960s of hosting free summer concerts for the public to enjoy. Neighbors regularly walk their dogs through the park, and sports teams play on the ballfields. While you're walking the grassy field, your mind may register something that seems out of place: fire hydrants. Only a few remain as remnants of the disturbing story of why what once existed here is no more.

This was the site of Reno City, a neighborhood of primarily Black residents. They had helped to construct the fort and used it for protection and to find employment during the Civil War. After the war, Black and white families were neighbors in modest houses and created a thriving community, including churches, stores, a Masonic Lodge where dances were held, a school, and a Black baseball team, the Fort Renos.

In the early 20th century, nearby white communities held contempt for the interracial, working-class Reno City and began to push for the government to acquire the land from 370 families and turn it into a park and schools for white children. They succeeded in getting District and federal officials to pass legislation to erase the neighborhood. Homeowners who did not agree to sell were threatened with condemnation. Many residents had trouble finding new homes they could afford with what they had been paid. The former Reno School built in 1903 for Black children was declared a historic landmark and restored in 2014 as a wing of the Alice Deal Middle School.

Address 4000 Chesapeake Street NW, Washington, DC 20016, www.nps.gov/places/fort-reno.htm | Getting there Metro to Tenlcytown (Red Line); bus 31, 31, N2 to Wisconsin Avenue & Chesapeake Street NW | Hours Daily dawn–dusk | Tip A few of the Reno City residents re-established themselves with the St. George's Episcopal Church in the Bloomingdale neighborhood (160 U Street NW, www.stgeorgedc.org).

41 Foxcroft Heights Park

First taste of freedom

The years during and after the Civil War brought with them the necessity to provide housing for thousands of formerly enslaved individuals struggling to meet their basic needs. In 1863, the Federal Government established Freedman's Village on land that had been a plantation and would become Arlington National Cemetery in 1864. The idea was to create a model planned community for formerly enslaved people, where they could achieve self-sufficiency with the provision of homes, medical and social services, and education. Two famous Black Americans who helped support Freedman's Village were Elizabeth Keckley (1818–1907), dressmaker to Mary Todd Lincoln, and Sojourner Truth (1797–1883), abolitionist, women's rights activist, and preacher.

Life was not easy here due to a style of military rule set up by the Army and later the Bureau of Refugees, Freedmen, and Abandoned Lands. But it offered a level of freedom and opportunity that many who came to live here had never experienced. This community of freed Black people was originally planned as a temporary solution to the social issues of the day. The government tried to shut it down several times, but these efforts were met with protests from the residents who wished to stay. Freedman's Village was finally closed in 1898. Residents were given a monetary stipend to leave their homes, and some of them established new neighborhoods nearby.

Foxcroft Heights Park is a small, neighborhood park in Arlington, Virginia that is located just south of Arlington National Cemetery. Look for two markers that commemorate the history of Freedman's Village, which was located in the part of the cemetery that you can see from here. The park offers benches, picnic tables, and a play area for young children. It also boasts a beautiful view of the nearby US Air Force Memorial, the US Capitol building, and surrounding Washington, DC.

FREEDMAN'S VILLAGE

AFTER THE OUTBREAK OF THE CIVIL WAR, ESCAPED SLAVES SOUGHT REFUGE AT UNION CAMPS AND THOUSANDS CROWDED INTO THE FEDERAL CITY. IN RESPONSE TO THE UNHEALTHY CONDITIONS IN WASHINGTON, THE GOVERNMENT SELECTED A SITE ON ARLINGTON HEIGHTS IN MAY, 1863, TO PROVIDE FREED SLAVES WITH HOUSING AND OPPORTUNITIES FOR WORK, TRAINING AND EDUCATION. FREEDMAN'S VILLAGE, WHICH WAS LOCATED IN ARLINGTON NATIONAL CEMETERY, WAS SOON BUILT AND FORMALLY DEDICATED ON DECEMBER 4, 1863. THERE WERE OVER 50 TWO-STORY DUPLEX HOUSES, TWO CHURCHES, A SCHOOL, A MEETING HALL, HOSPITAL AND HOME FOR THE AGED AND INFIRM. IN TIME THE POPULATION EXCEEDED 1,000. THOUGH INTENDED TO BE TEMPORARY, THE VILLAGE LASTED INTO THE 1890s, WHEN IT WAS CLOSED AND ITS RESIDENTS DISPERSED.

ERECTED BY ARLINGTON COUNTY, VIRGINIA

801 S Oak Street, Arlington, VA 22204, www.arlingtoncemetery.mil/Explore/History-of-Arlington-National-Cemetery/Freedmans-Village   Bus 16A, 16C, 16E, 16M to Southgate Road & Air Force Memorial Drive   Daily dawn–dusk   Lewis Jefferson (1866–1946) was one of the city's first Black millionaires. He owned several businesses, including steamboats that transported guests to the amusement park he developed on the Potomac River. Look for the plaque that tells his story at the DC wharf (7th & Water Streets NW).

42 Frederick Douglass Historic Site

The sage of Anacostia

Washington, DC celebrated the reopening of the Frederick Douglass National Historic Site on July 4, 2023 after a closure of three and a half years. Secure your timed tickets online for guided tours of the home of the famous abolitionist, author, orator, and statesman. A brief video in the Visitor Center sets the stage.

Frederick Douglass (1818–1895) lived in this home from 1877 until his death. He named his estate Cedar Hill for its high elevation and bountiful trees. Douglas certainly would have enjoyed the view of the Federal City from his front porch. His wife Anna Murray died in 1882. Douglass married Helen Pitts in 1884 and lived here with her. The estate home is set on beautiful grounds, where a small farm and a peach orchard once stood. Behind the house is a replica of his "Growlery," a small stone cabin he used as his refuge for thinking and writing.

The tour gives a personal glimpse into Douglass's life through several original artifacts. You'll walk the 21-room mansion, including the parlors, dining room, kitchen, and bedrooms. His love of art and family is evident in pictures displayed throughout the home. Make sure to see the mysterious paw print set in concrete in a back room that was likely from a family dog. The tropical themed wallpaper is a replica of a gift given to him by the Haitian President Florvil Hyppolite when he served as the US ambassador there (1889–1891).

Here at home, Douglass lived a full life, from discussing issues of the day with reporters to giving piggyback rides to his grandchildren. He enjoyed nature and would collect flowers, plants, and artifacts from the grounds or on walks along the Anacostia River, and then he'd press them into books or use them for decorations. His legacy of persistence continues to inspire millions.

Address 1411 W Street SE, Washington, DC 20020, +1 (202) 426-5961, www.nps.gov/frdo/ index.htm, frdo_visitorservices@nps.gov | Getting there Bus B2, V2 to 14th & W Streets SE | Hours See website for seasonal hours | Tip View contemporary works by a variety of artists in historic Anacostia at the Honfleur gallery, which hosts a rigorous schedule of exhibitions and programming focusing on cutting-edge contemporary exhibitions by artists from east of the Anacostia River, the United States, and abroad (1241 Good Hope Road SE, www.honfleurgallerydc.com).

43 Freedom House Museum
Fiendish and shocking

Freedom House Museum is what remains of a slave market, where one of the largest slave trading firms in the country forcibly held enslaved people to await transport south to a future of hard labor on cotton plantations. Tens of thousands of men, women, and children were trafficked here during the years 1828-1861. The exhibits tell the local stories of the slave trade, the military, and families.

"Behold ... the American slave-trade ... Tell me citizens, WHERE, under the sun, you can witness a spectacle more fiendish and shocking". Frederick Douglass, orator and abolitionist, spoke these words in 1852 during his famous speech, "What to the Slave is the Fourth of July." The audience was the Ladies Anti-Slavery Society of Rochester in New York State, where he worked as editor of an anti-slavery publication.

A blown-up photograph on the main level of this townhouse shows that the facility was once much larger. Two 14-foot-high, concrete walls were the front of the "slave pens" on either side of the building, one for men and one for women and children, and they kept the people inside separated from the outside world. They were chained to each other and to the floors at night.

Several stories of local Alexandria residents are told within the museum. One of those stories is about the man in whose honor the museum was named. Lewis Henry Bailey was one of the enslaved children sold here. As a young boy, he was torn away from his mother Ann and ended up in Texas. Once he received his freedom in 1863 during the last years of the Civil War, he walked all the way back to Virginia to find his mother, who was living not far from the former slave market's location. Along the way, he received the calling to be a minister and founded five churches and two schools during his lifetime. His daughter, Annie B. Rose, preserved the family history, and you can see her treasured typewriter on display in the museum.

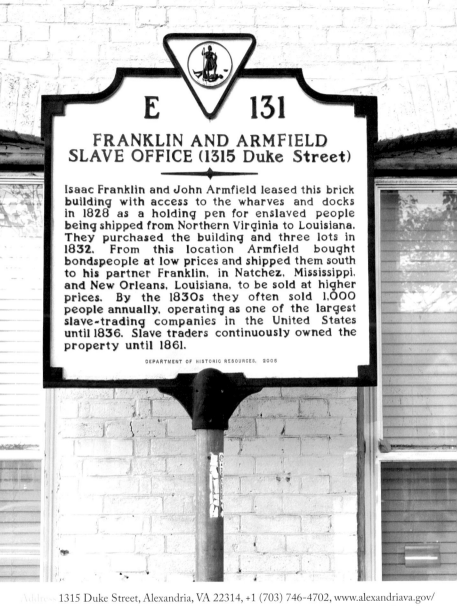

E 131

FRANKLIN AND ARMFIELD
SLAVE OFFICE (1315 Duke Street)

Isaac Franklin and John Armfield leased this brick building with access to the wharves and docks in 1828 as a holding pen for enslaved people being shipped from Northern Virginia to Louisiana. They purchased the building and three lots in 1832. From this location Armfield bought bondspeople at low prices and shipped them south to his partner Franklin, in Natchez, Mississippi, and New Orleans, Louisiana, to be sold at higher prices. By the 1830s they often sold 1,000 people annually, operating as one of the largest slave-trading companies in the United States until 1836. Slave traders continuously owned the property until 1861.

DEPARTMENT OF HISTORIC RESOURCES, 2005

Address 1315 Duke Street, Alexandria, VA 22314, +1 (703) 746-4702, www.alexandriava.gov/FreedomHouse Getting there Metro to King Street-Old Town (Blue, Yellow Lines) Hours Thu & Fri 11am–4pm, Sat 11am–5pm, Sun & Mon 1–5pm Tip Brighten your day with a visit to Puppet Heaven, located in the Crystal City Shops and owned by Alban Odoulamy, formally trained puppeteer. The shop features many unique and more familiar characters that will bring back memories (1675-O Crystal Square Arcade, Arlington, VA, www.thecrystalcityshops.com).

44 Freedom Plaza Hand Dancing

Hand dancing, the official dance of DC

Freedom Plaza is named in honor of Dr. Martin Luther King, Jr., who finished his "I Have a Dream" speech at the nearby Willard Hotel. On the floor of the plaza is a map of the original layout of the city, a time capsule containing items that belonged to Dr. King that will be opened in 2088, and several quotes from famous Americans. One such quote from editor Benjamin McKelway on the plaza reads, "There are two Washingtons – political Washington and the real Washington made up of friends and neighbors."

Each spring, the plaza becomes a place where friends and neighbors gather to enjoy music, hand dancing, and urban line dancing. Hand dancing is a form of partner dancing derived from the Lindy Hop, also known as "fast dancing" by the countless locals who grew up dancing in this style at clubs, house parties, and backyard barbecues. It was also designated as the official dance of Washington, DC in a 1999 proclamation by the DC City Council. Earl Pope, the president of the National Hand Dance Association at that time, said, "Receiving the official status was a big step in helping to preserve this form of dance. I hope to see its legacy continued by younger generations."

Several years ago, native Washingtonian and avid hand dancer Joe Jackson had a vision for a place in the city where seniors could go for a safe and enjoyable night out. So he organized this popular, ongoing, weekly event. Jackson passed away in 2021, but his family is keeping his vision alive on Freedom Plaza. His brother Keith handles the management, and brother Mike is the lead DJ, playing primarily R&B from the Motown era. Keith believes his brother is smiling down from above at each event. "The plaza is open to everyone, and all you need to do is bring a lawn chair and come out to have a good time," says Keith. "We will keep this yearly celebration going for as long as we can."

Address 1455 Pennsylvania Avenue NW, Washington, DC 20004 | Getting there Metro to Federal Triangle or Smithsonian (Blue, Orange, Silver Lines); bus 32, 33, 36, 52, 11Y, 16E, DC3 to 14th Street & Pennsylvania Avenue NW | Hours Jun–Oct Wed 6–9pm | Tip WOOK-TV, the first all-Black television station in the nation, was on the air from 1963 to 1972 and hosted the "Teenarama Dance Party," DC's first Black teen dance show. View the plaque on the front far left corner of the building and see the link for story and video (5321 1st Place NE, www.dancepartytheteenaramastory.com).

45 Glen Echo Park

Today, the fun is for everyone

Glen Echo Park was established in 1891 as an educational and cultural center, and it would later become a fully functioning amusement park. Attendance peaked in the early 1920s and late 1930s. Families and friends came here to enjoy movies, a wooden roller coaster, a scenic railway, the Crystal Pool that could accommodate 3,000 swimmers, and a carousel, complete with 52 wooden circus animals swirling to happy music. But not everyone could enjoy this joyful place. The privately-owned park was segregated, and Black people were barred from entering.

In 1960, a group of Howard University students organized protests and, along with others, pressured the park to end its segregated practices. On June 30, 1960, the students held a sit-in on the carousel. They were arrested for "criminal trespass," and their case went all the way to the US Supreme Court, which overturned the arrests in 1964. The amusement park was desegregated in 1961 until it closed permanently to visitors in 1968. The National Park Service took over management of the site in 1970 and transferred the role to Montgomery County, Maryland in 2002, in partnership with a dedicated non-profit organization.

Today, there are many attractions for everyone, including art studios and galleries, where you can often find resident artists at work. Go swing dancing with a free dance lesson in the beautiful and historic Spanish Ballroom, or take one of the many visual or performing arts classes. You can also enjoy the carousel and aquarium, children's theaters, a playground, picnic areas, and the Praline Café.

In 2023, the park hosted its first annual Juneteenth celebration, and some of the original protestors returned to share their memories and to take a ceremonial ride on the carousel. Look for the bronze marker near the carousel that recounts their story, and an upcoming documentary about the civil rights history of the park.

Address 7300 MacArthur Boulevard, Glen Echo, MD 20812, +1 (301) 634-2222, www.glenechopark.org, info@glenechopark.org | Getting there Metro to Bethesda (Red Line), then transfer to bus 29 to MacArthur Boulevard & Goldsboro Road | Hours Grounds daily 6am – 1am, check website for venue hours | Tip On August 28, 1963, during the historic March on Washington for Jobs and Freedom, the Gwynn Oak Amusement Park in Baltimore, Maryland ended its policy of segregation, and an 11-month-old Black girl took her first ride. The carousel is being renovated, and it will return to the National Mall, right outside the Smithsonian Castle, for the nation's 250th anniversary in 2026 (1000 Jefferson Drive SW, www.smithsonian.com/carousel).

46 *The Green Book* at NMAAHC

A historic road trip

Road trips have been a staple of American life for decades. And no road trip was ever complete without some of Mom's home cooking, including fried chicken, potato salad, and other picnic fare. But in the Jim Crow era, a trip to visit relatives in another state was not carefree for Black Americans, which meant that bringing certain items, like an ice chest, pillows, and anything else you may need on the road, was essential. White business owners could legally turn away Black travelers seeking a meal, a room for the night, or even a restroom.

Victor H. Green was a postal worker born and raised in New York. After hearing first-hand stories about threats and discrimination, he decided to create a travel guide for Black travelers.

The Green Book, published from 1937 through 1966, helped Black people safely navigate the hostile and racist environments of the Jim Crow era. The guide with the green cover helped them find restaurants, hotels, beauty salons, and gas stations. It also provided guidance about packing food, water, blankets, and even empty cans for when finding a restroom was not an option.

Experience *The Green Book* at the Smithsonian's National Museum of African American History and Culture (NMAAHC). At the Blue Cadillac on Level L2 in the *Follow the Green Book* exhibit, you'll use an interactive touchscreen to get ready for a trip and to make important decisions about your route and the places you'll stop.

Green noted, "There will be a day sometime in the near future when this guide will not have to be published. That is when we as a race will have equal opportunities and privileges in the United States." Green died in 1960, four years before the passage of the Civil Rights Act of 1964 that prohibited discrimination based on race, creed, color, religion, sex, or national origin in the US.

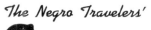

Green Book

The Negro Travelers'

Address 1400 Constitution Avenue NW, Washington, DC 20560, +1 (844) 750-3012, www.nmaahc.si.edu | Getting there Metro to Federal Triangle (Blue, Orange, Silver Lines); bus 52, 11Y, 16E to 14th Street & Constitution Avenue NW; DC Circulator to 15th Street & Jefferson Drive NW (National Mall Line) | Hours Mon noon–5:30pm, Tue–Sun 10am–5:30pm | Tip On February 1, 1960, four Black college students sat down at a "whites only" Woolworth counter in Greensboro, North Carolina. They were asked to leave due to racial segregation, but they remained in their seats and ignited a movement to challenge inequality. See that very counter at the Smithsonian Museum of American History (1300 Constitution Avenue NW, www.americanhistory.si.edu).

47 __ Healey Hall

Race, place and privilege at Georgetown University

Patrick Francis Healy (1834–1990) served as Georgetown University's (GU) president between 1873 and 1882. He was born on a plantation in Macon, Georgia to a wealthy, Catholic-Irish father and an enslaved mother. By Georgia law, he was classified as enslaved, but he was able to escape the indignities associated with that label when his father sent him and his siblings north. Healey enrolled at Holy Cross College in Massachusetts, and his father's friend Bishop John Fitzpatrick looked after him. Healy had fair skin, and he appeared to be European, which allowed him to "pass" as white.

Jesuits believed in his abilities and helped him conceal his heritage. Healy himself referenced it in a letter to his friend recalling, "Remarks are sometimes made… which wound my very heart. You know to what I refer." After schooling abroad, he was assigned to GU, an institution that had been built by enslaved persons. It was also rescued from financial ruin by the 1838 sale of 272 enslaved persons. In 2019, a collaboration including Jesuits and the descendants of the enslaved, representing more than 10,000 ancestors, came together to create the Descendants Truth & Reconciliation Foundation and commit funds to address and heal the wounds associated with this history at GU and across the United States. Healy is buried in the University's Jesuit cemetery.

Healy made significant changes that modernized the school. He added science and physics to the curriculum and expanded the schools of law and medicine. He also oversaw construction of the flagship building on campus, later named in his honor. Healy Hall is a Victorian-style, four-story building with a central spire that rises 200 feet above the ground. The building once included an indoor track, a bowling alley, and an air raid shelter. GU has plans to transform the ground floor into a student center with resources to support student success.

Address 37th & O Streets NW, Washington, DC 20057, +1 (202) 687-0100, www.facilities. georgetown.edu/healy-hall | **Getting there** Bus G2 to 37th & O Streets NW | **Tip** Emma V. Brown (1840–1902), a native Washingtonian, was the first Black teacher employed by the DC Public Schools. Educated at Myrtilla Miner's school, and at Oberlin College, she opened a private school for neighborhood children in her own home (3044 P Street NW).

48 Howard University Gallery of Art

Hattie's come home

Howard University was chartered in 1867, shortly after the Civil War ended. Howard is one of the most well-known and respected Historically Black Colleges and Universities (HBCUs) for its legacy of producing top African American talent and scholars. Art in all its forms is an integral part of the institution, which, like many other HBCUs, has a history of nurturing and supporting Black artists.

The Gallery of Art was established in 1870 and houses one of the most impressive collections in the art world. It's located in the Chadwick Boseman School of Fine Arts in Lulu Vere Childers Hall and features rotating exhibits of contemporary arts and crafts. Stop by regularly to see the new exhibitions, and while you're there, ask the staff for directions to another location in the building to view a mural that most people don't know about. It was commissioned by Howard's president more than 20 years ago and brings alive the spirit of music as practiced by Howard students over the years.

In 1940, Hattie McDaniel was the first Black actor to receive an Academy Award for her 1939 role in *Gone With The Wind*. Her last will and testament bequeathed the award to Howard, but decades ago, the Oscar mysteriously disappeared from the school. In October 2023, the Academy of Motion Picture Arts and Sciences presented the university with a replacement to honor the late actor's wishes. The award, along with a letter to McDaniel's family and a picture of the actor will remain on permanent display. Dean Phylicia Rashad spoke at an event to mark the occasion. She reflected on her time as a student at Howard and how the original Oscar was in a room where she had classes. She said the award is an "affirmation and a presence" for students, as if McDaniels were sitting right there with them.

Address 2455 6th Street NW, First Floor, Washington, DC 20059, +1 (202) 806-7040, finearts.howard.edu | Getting there Metro to Shaw/Howard University (Green Line); bus 79 to Georgia Avenue & Howard Place NW, or bus 70 to Georgia Avenue & Euclid Street NW | Hours Mon–Fri 10am–4pm | Tip *Bearing Witness* is a 40-foot, 20,000-pound, bronze sculpture by world-renowned artist and DC native Martin Puryear. The shape is based on the ceremonial wooden *ngil* masks historically used by the Fang people in the African nation of Gabon (Woodrow Wilson Plaza, 1300 Pennsylvania Avenue NW, www.gsa.gov).

49 HR Records
Embracing the sounds of DC culture

There was a magic that millions experienced before digital music came into existence. It was the moment a new band or artist released music, and you had to go into a record store to buy it on vinyl. The anticipation leading up to the release was electric. The experience was about music, but there was much more to it than that. It was about culture and community.

"Historically, record shops, even barber shops have been a place where the community comes to listen, to talk, and to exchange ideas about what's going on and I think we've created that space," says HR Records owner Charvis Campbell.

Campbell describes himself as a husband, father, and record lover. He's a Howard University graduate, who formerly worked as an associate dean at George Mason University. He never planned to open a record store. But when a shop he frequented was going out of business, the owner convinced him to buy the entire inventory. He ended up with about 5,000 records and no plan, and that's how HR records began. "HR" is short for Home Rule, which is a track on legendary DC-born jazz flutist Lloyd McNeill's album *Washington Suite* and a reference to DC's lack of autonomy in government.

HR features blues, jazz, soul, R&B, Go-Go, Hip-Hop and International, the music that tells the story of music in DC. The store is filled with bins of music. Records line the walls, and staff will talk with you about your interests or just let you browse. Vice President Kamala Harris famously visited HR Records in 2023, purchasing records by Charles Mingus and Roy Ayers, and the *Porgy and Bess* soundtrack.

The Home Rule Music and Film Preservation Foundation, co-founded by Campbell and Michael Bernstein, is a non-profit, multimedia arts and education organization that sponsors the popular, family-friendly Home Rule Music Festival each June at the Parks at Walter Reed, celebrating DC's music and culture.

Address 702 Kennedy Street NW, Washington, DC 20011, +1 (202) 469-9868, www.homerulerecords.com | Getting there Bus E4 to 7th & Kennedy Streets NW | Hours Mon–Fri 2–8pm, Sat noon–8pm, Sun noon–6pm | Tip Stop by Büna Coffeehouse to enjoy authentic rich flavors of Ethiopian coffee and cuisine (4400 Georgia Avenue NW, www.bunacoffeehouse.com).

50 International Spy Museum

Spying that shaped history

Many know the story of Harriet Tubman's bravery in escaping a life of slavery, only to return to the South 13 times to lead more than 70 enslaved people along the Underground Railroad to freedom. Lesser known is her work as a spy for the Union Army during the Civil War and her role as the first woman in US history to lead a military expedition.

Harriet Tubman wanted to ensure freedom for all enslaved people and realized that war was necessary to make this a reality. So she traveled to South Carolina in the Spring of 1862 to help the Union Army. In 1863, Tubman was recruited to become head of a spy ring. With a network of enslaved and free people who knew the local waterways and byways, she gathered crucial intelligence about Confederate supply routes, ammunition, and troop movements.

In June of that year, Tubman oversaw an expedition carrying Black troops along the Combahee River into Confederate territory. The intelligence she gathered allowed the ships to proceed unharmed because they knew where Confederate mines had been submerged. During the raid, Union soldiers burned plantations, fields, barns, and storehouses. Slave owners and Confederate soldiers were overwhelmed and powerless in trying to regain order. Enslaved people ran towards the ships, and more than 700 sailed to freedom.

Tubman sought compensation for her services during the war but was denied, since her services as a nurse, cook, spy, and scout were not documented. All she had received was $200 for three years of service. Thirty-four years later, she would get a small pension as the widow of a soldier she married after the war.

The International Spy Museum has an exhibit that details Harriet Tubman's efforts. Look for the stories of more African American spies, such as James Lafayette, Josephine Baker, Robert Smalls, Malcolm Nance, Debra Evans Smith, and Darrell M. Blocker.

Address 700 L'Enfant Plaza SW, Washington, DC 20024, +1 (202) 393-7798, www.spymuseum.org, info@spymuseum.org | Getting there Metro to L'Enfant Plaza (Blue, Green, Orange, Silver, Yellow Lines); bus 51 to 12th & C Streets SW; DC Circulator to 7th & D Streets SW (Eastern Market-L'Enfant Plaza Line) | Hours Tue–Fri 10am–6pm, Sat 9am–7pm, Sun & Mon 9am–6pm | Tip The exuberant performer, civil rights activist, and World War II spy for the French Resistance Josephine Baker was one of only a few women on the podium overlooking the Reflecting Pool at the Lincoln Memorial during the 1968 March on Washington for Jobs and Freedom (2 Lincoln Memorial Circle NW).

51 John Lewis Mural

Get in trouble. Good trouble.

John Lewis (1940-2020) was a pioneer in the fight for civil rights. This minister, lawyer, and congressman was born in Troy, Alabama to humble beginnings as the child of a sharecropper. He spent his early years being educated in segregated schools.

From a young age, Lewis wanted to be a minister and used the family livestock as his congregation. He would preach to his chickens, and he once joked that his first act of nonviolent protest was refusing to eat the birds.

Inspired by Rosa Parks' refusal to give up her seat on an Alabama bus, Lewis later corresponded with Dr. Martin Luther King, Jr. and became active in the Civil Rights Movement. At 23, he led the Student Nonviolent Coordinating Committee (SNCC) and was the youngest speaker to address 250,000 people at the March on Washington for Jobs and Freedom on August 28, 1963.

In 1965, he famously led what was supposed to be a peaceful march of 600 across the Edmund Pettus Bridge in Selma, Alabama in support of voting rights. The march was stopped by police violence and later became known as "Bloody Sunday." This event galvanized public opinion and mobilized Congress to pass the Voting Rights Act, which was signed into law on August 6, 1965.

Lewis' mother often told him to stay out of trouble. "But I told her that I got into a good trouble, necessary trouble," he said. "Even today, I tell people, 'We need to get in good trouble.'"

At the site of HIS Grooming, where Lewis was an occasional client, are two black and white murals honoring him. One features his distinctive face and his "Good Trouble" message. The other depicts Lewis in a barbershop chair in conversation with his younger self. Black-owned barbershops have long served as social clubs where Black men can talk openly about nationwide and community issues in a safe and welcoming space – and pass on wisdom to younger generations.

Address 1242 Pennsylvania Avenue SE, Washington, DC 20003 | Getting there Metro to Potomac Avenue (Blue Line); bus 32, 36 to Pennsylvania Avenue & 13th Street SE | Hours Unrestricted | Tip *Journey Anacostia*, by local sculptor Wilfredo Valladares, is a tribute to the culture, history, and spirit of the Anacostia community (1201 Good Hope Road & Martin Luther King, Jr. Avenue SE, www.wilfredovalladares.com/journey-anacostia).

Josh Gibson Statue
at Nationals Park

Possibly the greatest hitter in baseball

Nationals Park is home to the 2019 World Series Champion Washington Nationals professional baseball team. Opened in 2008, the nearly 42,000-seat ballpark is part of the ongoing revitalization of the waterfront south of the Capitol into the mixed-use Capitol Riverfront neighborhood. According to MLB.com, inspiration for the look of the stadium was taken from the East Wing of the National Gallery of Art.

Outside the Home Plate Gate at Nationals Stadium, you are greeted by bronze statues of DC baseball icons, one of whom is Josh Gibson (1911-1947), star player for the Washington-area Homestead Grays. He was one of the most powerful hitters and catchers in the history of the game and also a Black man. The Grays were one of the teams in the former Negro Leagues that existed from the 1920s through the mid 1940s. All of the players were Black athletes who were subject to an unofficial "color line" that did not allow them to play on white teams. The team split their time between Forbes Field in Pittsburgh and Griffith Stadium in DC, now the site of Howard University Hospital.

In 1972, Gibson was inducted into the illustrious Baseball Hall of Fame in Cooperstown, New York. His plaque reads in part, "Considered greatest slugger in Negro Baseball Leagues, power hitting catcher who hit almost 800 home runs in league and independent baseball during his 17-year career." For reference, Babe Ruth hit 714 home runs in his career, followed by Hank Aaron with 755, and then Barry Bonds with 762. Gibson was unquestionably one of the greatest players of all time.

Josh Gibson died shortly before Jackie Robinson signed with the Brooklyn Dodgers in April 1947. Robinson was the first Black player in the major leagues after 63 years and essentially broke the "color line."

1500 S Capitol Street SE, Washington, DC 20003, +1 (202) 675-6287, www.mlb.com
Metro to Navy Yard-Ballpark (Green Line); bus 74 to O & Half Streets SE;
DC Circulator to M & Half Streets SE (Eastern Market L'Enfant Plaza Line)   Daily
dusk–dawn   Just a few steps inside of the lobby of Howard University Hospital is an
outline showing where home plate and the batter's boxes once stood in the old stadium where
the Homestead Grays and Washington Senators played (2041 Georgia Avenue NW).

53 Josiah Henson Museum & Park

The fallacy of Uncle Tom

Josiah Henson was a virtuous man. He was no "Uncle Tom," the derogatory term that became popular in the early 1900s for a Black man who would betray his race. Henson's 1849 autobiography, *The Life of Josiah Henson, Formerly a Slave, Now an Inhabitant of Canad*a, details his life on the Riley plantation and the brutality and suffering he endured there. His book inspired Harriet Beecher Stowe's landmark anti-slavery novel, *Uncle Tom's Cabin* (1852). In her book, a fictional enslaved man named Uncle Tom, characterized as trustworthy and hardworking, is beaten to death in the end on the order of his enslaver for not revealing the whereabouts of other enslaved people. The negative caricature of this man that emerged over time came from minstrel shows and racist advertisements.

Henson was born into slavery in 1789 in Charles County, Maryland. His father was sold down South, and Henson was later separated from his mother and siblings in a slave auction. He reunited with his mother years later on the Riley Plantation, where he remained for 30 years. In 1830, he escaped with his wife and children to Canada. He would go on to establish the Dawn Settlement for the formerly enslaved that included a school and a lumber mill. Henson risked his life to return to the US several times and free 188 people on the Underground Railroad. He became a celebrity and traveled the world telling his story, including visits with President Hayes and Queen Victoria. Josiah Henson died in 1883 at the age of 94, leaving behind 8 children, 44 grandchildren, and 6 great-grandchildren.

The Josiah Henson Museum & Park contains the historic home and its attached log kitchen. You will experience Rev. Henson's life through multimedia exhibits. Up to 50,000 artifacts have been discovered on the property, including one of the Riley's chamber pots.

Address 11410 Old Georgetown Road, North Bethesda, MD 20852, +1 (301) 765-8790, www.josiahhenson.org | Getting there Metro to North Bethesda (Red Line); bus 26 to Old Georgetown Road & Tilden Lane | Hours Fri & Sat 10am–4pm, Sun noon–4pm | Tip The Sandy Spring Slave Museum & African Art Gallery highlights the heritage of Black families in Montgomery County, the significant contributions that African Americans have made in building the nation, the struggle of civil rights, and more through an extensive collection of historical art and artifacts (18524 Brooke Road, Sandy Spring, MD, www.sandyspringslavemuseum.org).

54 KanKouran West African Dance Company

Celebrating the universal language of dance

A visit to KanKouran West African Dance Company makes you feel like you've been transported across the seas, but without a 20+ hour flight. When you enter the building there are authentic African items for sale including clothing, jewelry, and accessories. Head into the large dance studio, kick off your shoes and join one of the most fun and energetic workouts you've ever experienced. Students, many dressed in colorful African attire, form lines that stretch across the dance floor and repeat dance patterns demonstrated by the instructor to the polyrhythmic beats of live drummers. People of all ages and all abilities are welcome.

The lively dance class is led by Assane Konte, Co-Founder and Artistic Director of KanKouran and a native of Senegal, West Africa. "It serves as an educational institution designed to preserve the dance culture of the Senegal-Gambia region of Africa through performances and educational programs," says Konte.

Konte began his dance training at age 12 and has studied with prominent dancers and musicians from multiple countries. He started dancing professionally at the age of 15 with the Ballet Africaine de Diebel Guee of Dakar, Senegal. During his 10 years with the company, he electrified audiences with his highly energetic performances, while simultaneously developing his own unique movement style. Konte started KanKouran in 1983 after leaving Africa to pursue his dream of establishing his own dance company in the nation's capital.

KanKouran holds a concert production in the Washington area as part of its widely acclaimed, annual public conference during Labor Day weekend. Konte and his dancers have performed across the US and around the world and collaborated with countless organizations, including the Kennedy Center.

Address Dance Exchange, 7117 Maple Avenue, Takoma Park, MD 20912, +1 (202) 518-1213, www.kankouran.org | Getting there Metro to Takoma (Red Line); bus 12, 13, 16, 8, 25 to Carrol & Maple Avenues | Hours See website for class and event schedules | Tip While in Maryland, take a walk along the popular and scenic Matthew Henson Trail in Matthew Henson Memorial Park, dedicated to the famous explorer who was arguably the first man to set foot at the North Pole during his trek with Robert E. Peary (Charles & Edgebrook Roads, Silver Spring, MD, www.mongtgomerycountyparks.org).

55 __ Kitchen + Kocktails

Kevin Kelley elevates comfort food for DC

Kitchen + Kocktails by Kevin Kelley opened in 2023, and within months it became one of the most booked restaurants in the entire DC area, according to reservation service OpenTable. "The people of DC have always been kind and welcoming, and they love their city," says Kelley, who has family ties to the area. "And in my other restaurants across the country we've had a number of guests from the city who have said that we need this restaurant in DC." Kelley, a lawyer and the first of his family to own a business, is thankful that the people of DC have embraced Kitchen + Kocktails, which also allowed him to provide 125 jobs for Black employees in the culinary field.

Upon entering the space, you'll face a wall covered in hundreds of red roses. There is a full-service bar and a large, beautifully styled dining room. This is a place to see and be seen, with urban music and a nightclub feel. The combination of food and drinks makes for an unforgettable experience. "I can promise you that there is no one in the country that makes food as good as my chefs make it," says Kelley.

The restaurant specializes in elevated comfort food, with dishes like southern fried chicken and catfish, lobster tail, shrimp and grits, salmon, pork chops, and a variety of creative appetizers. Portions are large, and you'll likely take home enough for another meal for the next day. Sides are purchased separately, and you can finish your dining experience with desserts that include bread pudding, peach cobbler, and banana pudding.

Indulge in one of their astonishing "kreative kocktails," like the "Cotton Candy Cloud" made with freshly spun cotton candy that melts upon a pour of Ciroc Summer Citrus. The "Gold Fashioned" is mixed tableside and unveiled in a cloud of smoke before being topped with edible gold flakes. Or try the delicious blackberry margarita topped with rock candy.

Address 1300 I Street NW, Washington, DC 20005, +1 (202) 998-6538, www.kitchenkocktailsusa.com | Getting there Metro to McPherson Square (Blue, Orange, Silver Lines); bus 80, D6, G8, S2, S9, X2 to Franklin Square Bus Bay A | Hours Sun 10am–10pm, Mon–Thu 11am–10pm, Fri 11am–11pm, Sat 10am–11pm | Tip Sankofa Video, Books and Café was founded by Shirikiana and Haile Gerima for thoughtful consideration of the past and future through books, films, and programming particularly generated by and about people of African descent. Join their open mic nights the last Friday of each month (2714 Georgia Avenue NW, www.sankofa.com).

56_Lady Clipper Barber Shop
A passion for precision

Lesley "Lady Clipper" Bryant was born in Trinidad and raised in DC. If you had asked her what she wanted to be when she grew up, the answer would likely not have been, "Barber." That would have been a glimpse into a future she could not yet see.

But when her life demanded a change, Bryant accepted the challenge. Today, she owns the city's premier, full-service, woman-owned barbershop staffed by barbers who are women. The shop is bright and stylish, with gleaming red and chrome barber chairs, and relaxing music playing on the sound system. Works from local artists adorn the walls. The atmosphere is open and welcoming to all.

As a child helping her mother craft handmade dolls, Bryant knew that she would always love art and creativity. She studied design and spent 12 years working in graphic design for a commercial real estate firm. After being laid off, Bryant went to her barber, who encouraged her to think about the field of barbering. It was an appealing notion, and, as Bryant says, "The rest is history." She was able to funnel her love of people and passion for artistic expression into her shop, which she opened in 2017. She worked a year by herself to prove that her business could be successful, and then she began putting together her team.

In 2021, Bryant and several of the Lady Clipper barbers were interviewed on *The Kelly Clarkson Show*. Clarkson introduced Lady Clipper as "a super cool barber shop in DC unlike any I've heard of before." Bryant sought to create a place where female clients, especially those with children, would feel welcome and comfortable, along with her male clientele. So she built a team of female barbers, whose skills can shine in her space. The team is professional and works hard to ensure a comfortable experience for their customers. Services include cuts, cornrows, detangling, beard trims, shaves, and even cuts for kids.

Address 1514 U Street NW, Washington, DC 20009, +1 (202) 368-4603, www.theladyclipper.com, contact@theladyclipper.com | Getting there Metro to U Street/African American Civil War Memorial/Cardozo (Green Line); bus S9, S2, 90, 96 to 16th & U Streets NW | Hours By online appointment only | Tip 11:Eleven Gallery is owned by London born Nicola Charles, specializing in urban art from the United Kingdom (10 Florida Avenue NW, www.11elevengallery.com).

57   Lafayette Pointer Park

An important park in DC history

Lafayette Pointer Park is a hidden gem in a quiet residential neighborhood. A remodeled recreation center run by the DC Department of Parks and Recreation opened to the public in 2021. You'll find a splash park, basketball courts, and tennis courts. There are play areas for kids, with lots of structures to climb on, swing from, and crawl through. One structure is nicknamed "the elephant" because of its large size and trunk-shaped slide. There are picnic tables and trails to walk and enjoy the outdoors.

The name Pointer was added with the re-opening in honor of Captain George Pointer. Born into slavery in 1773, his family was among early Black landowners to settle here. They lived on this site for 80 years until 1928, when their homes were taken via eminent domain to build Lafayette Elementary School and Lafayette Park to serve the all-white community growing around them. Historic Chevy Chase DC is spearheading efforts to acknowledge and honor the heritage of those who once lived here.

Pointer played a significant role in building the C&O Canal. He first worked as an enslaved laborer but would later become the last superintendent engineer at Great Falls. His accomplishments include purchasing his freedom, owning property, and growing crops to sell at the market in Georgetown. He was also the captain of a fleet of boats that delivered stone to DC for construction of federal buildings, including the White House and the Capitol.

Pointer wrote an 11-page petition to the Chesapeake & Ohio Canal Company, dated September 5, 1829, to protest the new canal's construction path, which threatened to flood his property and dispossess his family. This document is preserved at the National Archives. Today, Wing Dam, the intake dam for the Potomac River that he oversaw, is the only consistently operational structure of the canal ruins at Great Falls Park, more than 200 years later.

Address 5900 33rd Street NW, Washington, DC 20015, +1 (202) 282-2206, www.dpr.dc.gov | Getting there Metro to Tenleytown (Red Line); bus E4 to McKinley & 33rd Streets NW | Hours Daily dawn–dusk | Tip At the front of the Katzen Arts Center on the campus of American University is 6.5-foot-high, 3,000-pound, abstract sculpture of three large round disks by renowned artist Frederick J. Eversley, who left an engineering position in the Apollo space program to study sculpture (4400 Massachusetts Avenue NW, www.american.edu/cas/katzen).

58 Langston Golf Course

Golfing game changers

Langston Golf Course, established in 1939, is the culmination of efforts by several individuals to establish more golf courses where Black people could enjoy a day out on the links. The course is named in honor of John Mercer Langston (1829–1897), who helped to establish Howard University's law school. He also served as the first president of the Virginia State University, and he became the first Black US congressman elected from the state of Virginia in 1888. Langston serves as the home course of the Royal Golf Club and the Wake Robin Golf Club, established here as the nation's first clubs for Black men and women.

In 1939, there were 5,209 golf facilities in the country with fewer than 20 open to Black golfers. In Washington, the city's only golf facility open to Black players was the nine-hole course located in what is now Constitution Gardens near the Lincoln Memorial.

In the late 1800s, golfers used to fashion tees out of wet sand. The invention of the wooden golf tee literally "changed the game," and, according to the US Golf Association, the first patent went to Dr. George Grant, a Black dentist who played golf in a meadow near his home. Langston is a unique urban course that has been described as challenging. It sits on the Anacostia River in a beautiful setting near the National Arboretum, so don't be surprised to spot wildlife during your play, or to see Metro subway cars passing on the rails overhead. On the right side of the par-5 third hole, there is an oak tree affectionately named the "Joe Louis Tree" because the heavy-weight champion is said to have hit it every time he played here.

Langston has a driving range, pro shop, and café that is open to everyone. Group and private lessons for players of all ages and skill levels are available throughout the year. Not a golfer? Stop by for a snack and simply enjoy this historic place, and what Langston deems the best breakfast in town.

Address 2600 Benning Road NE, Washington, DC 20002, +1 (202) 397-8638, www.playdcgolf.com/langston-golf-course **Getting there** Metro to Minnesota Avenue (Orange Line), transfer to bus X2 to 26th Street & Benning Road NE **Hours** Daily 7:30am–5pm **Tip** Woodlawn is a historic cemetery dating to the 1800s, where nearly 36,000 are buried, nearly all of them African American, including Congressman John Mercer Lewis, composer and violinist William Mercer Cook, Mary Edna Brown Coleman, a founder of Delta Sigma Theta sorority, and Sarah H. Meriwether Nutter, a founder of Alpha Kappa Alpha sorority (4611 Benning Road SE, www.woodlawndc.org).

59 Leonard Grimes Plaque
Paving a way towards freedom

Leonard Andrew Grimes (1815-1874) was born free but witnessed the cruelty of slavery while travelling to the South as a hired worker for an enslaver. After seeing this injustice, he committed himself to doing something to aid the fight for freedom. In the mid 1830s, once he had earned enough money, Grimes purchased horses and carriages and established a coach business. The business was successful, and Grimes transported passengers in and around Washington, DC and Virginia. This new profession also offered the perfect cover when he became a conductor on the Underground Railroad, helping countless freedom seekers reach northern states. In 1833, Grimes married his wife Octavia, and they eventually had four children: Emma, John, Leonard, and Julia. Little is known about his immediate family.

In 1840, Grimes was caught helping an enslaved woman and her children flee to the North. He was fined $100 and sentenced to two years' hard labor in a Richmond, Virginia prison. While imprisoned, he had a religious awakening and became a minister, sharing God's word with his jailers and fellow prisoners alike. After his release, Grimes and his family moved to the free state of Massachusetts, where they would remain. He became affiliated with the Twelfth Street Baptist Church, where he served as pastor for 25 years. He and his parishioners were active in abolitionist activities.

During the Civil War, Grimes joined other Black leaders lobbying to allow free and enslaved Black people to enlist in the Union Army. Their requests were met in 1863 with the creation of the 54th Massachusetts Infantry Regiment, the war's second Black regiment.

A plaque dedicated to Grimes' life was dedicated in 2007 by George Washington University students, and sits amongst the campus buildings in the spot where Grimes owned a home for 10 years in the mid-1800s.

H & 22nd Streets NW, Washington, DC 20052   Metro to Foggy Bottom-GWU (Blue, Orange, Silver Lines); bus 31, 32, 36 to 23rd & I Streets NW   Unrestricted   The Toni Morrison Society placed a Bench By The Road outside GWU's Lisner Auditorium to commemorate the end of segregation at the theater in 1947 (730 21st Street NW, www.tonimorrisonsociety.org/bench.html).

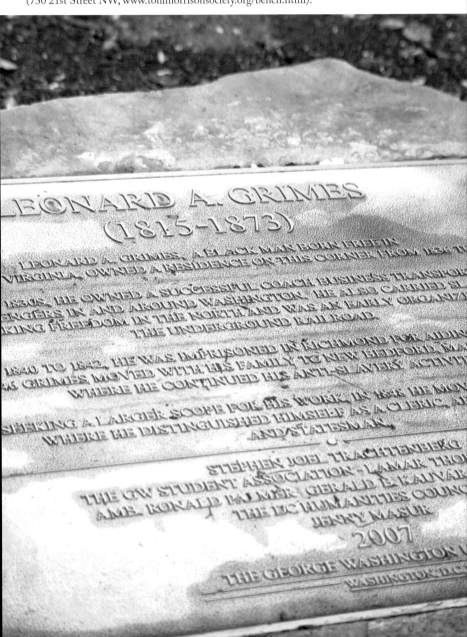

60 The Lincoln Memorial

A place to protest for freedom and equality

The Lincoln Memorial was built in honor of Abraham Lincoln (1809–1865), the 16th president of the United States. Following his death, he became known as the Great Emancipator for his efforts in ending slavery in the nation.

Architect Henry Bacon (1866–1924), who managed the design and construction of the memorial, selected the artist Jules Guérin (1866–1946) to adorn the memorial's interior with two murals, each 60 feet long and 12 feet high. The mural *Emancipation* sits on the south wall above the Gettysburg Address. It shows the Angel of Truth releasing enslaved people from the shackles of bondage. The left panel of the mural represents Justice and Law. The right panel represents Immortality. Surrounding the central figure are Faith, Hope, and Charity. The mural on the north wall above the Second Inaugural Address is *Unity*, representing the coming together of North and South. While Lincoln helped end slavery in the country, the fight for equality was just beginning. The 1922 dedication of the memorial was segregated by race.

Look for a marker on the spot where Martin Luther King, Jr. stood in front of 250,000 people during the March on Washington for Jobs and Freedom in 1963. Few people know or remember that this was not the first civil rights speech that Dr. King gave here.

Years earlier on May 17, 1957, people traveled for miles to attend the Prayer Pilgrimage for Freedom, organized by activist Bayard Rustin and others to protest the lack of progress in desegregating schools even though it was three years since the Supreme Court's decision in Brown vs. the Board of Education, which declared that school segregation was illegal. 25,000 people attended, making this the largest civil rights protest in the Nation's Capital at that time. Dr. Martin Luther King, Jr. gave the keynote speech at the event, which reinforced his role as a key leader in the civil rights movement.

Address 2 Lincoln Memorial Circle NW, Washington, DC 20037, +1 (202) 426-6841, www.nps.gov | Getting there Bus 3F to Constitution Avenue & 22nd Street NW; DC Circulator to Lincoln Memorial Circle (National Mall Line) | Hours Unrestricted | Tip President Lincoln's Cottage at the Soldier's Home is a historic site and museum in the place where he formulated his ideas on how to bring about an end to slavery and wrote the Emancipation Proclamation (140 Rock Creek Church Road NW, www.lincolncottage.org).

61 The Lincoln Theatre
A tale of two cities

"The movies end. The lights flash gaily on. The band down in the pit bursts into jazz. The crowd applauds a plump brown-skin bleached blonde who sings the troubles every woman has," from *Lincoln Theatre* by poet Langston Hughes.

These lines described any movie night at the Lincoln Theatre when it was a part of the U Street Corridor's flourishing Black Broadway, a "city" of Black Americans that existed when Washington, DC was segregated due to Jim Crow laws. Banks, bowling alleys, dance halls, movie houses, restaurants, skating rinks, and many other businesses were built for, managed by, or owned by Black Americans. It was the actress and singer Pearl Bailey who dubbed the neighborhood "Black Broadway," and the name stuck.

The Lincoln Theatre opened in 1922 as a silent movie house and Vaudeville site before becoming a luxury movie house in the late 1920s. The Lincoln Colonnade was the vibrant ballroom that opened in the basement of the venue. Performers there included luminaries such as Billie Holiday, Cab Calloway, Nat King Cole, Ella Fitzgerald, Lena Horne, and Sarah Vaughn. Even President Franklin Delano Roosevelt enjoyed the Lincoln Colonnade, which hosted two birthday balls in his honor, attracting megastars from Hollywood, including Louis Armstrong, Jimmy Stewart, Gene Kelly, Joe Louis, James Cagney, among many others.

As Washington, DC began to become integrated in the 1950s, Black families started patronizing formerly segregated businesses, which severely affected the U street economy. And much of the neighborhood sustained damage during the rioting that followed the assassination of Dr. Martin Luther King, Jr. in 1968. The Lincoln Theatre was then sold and closed for renovation in 1983, reopening only in 1994. Enjoy a wide variety of performances today at the historic theater, one of the few businesses still open since the days of Black Broadway.

Address 1215 U Street NW, Washington, DC 20009, +1 (202) 888-0050, www.thelincolndc.com, info@thelincolndc.com | Getting there Metro to U Street/African American Civil War Memorial/ Cardozo (Green, Yellow Lines); bus 90, 92 to 13th & U Streets NW, or bus 52, 54, 59 to 14th & U Streets NW | Hours See website for schedule | Tip The Industrial Bank of Washington was founded by Black businessman John Whitelaw Lewis in 1913. The U Street building was financed and built by Lewis and was the only Black-owned bank in the city at the time. The bank remains Black-owned, and you can still see the original architecture today (2000 11th Street NW, www.industrial-bank.com).

62 Mansion on O
& O Museum

Rosa Parks' home away from home

The Mansion on O is a place of surprise and delight. Behind an unassuming row-house door, this maze-like complex of five connected townhouses has over 100 themed rooms, 80 secret doors, and countless treasures, including art, collectibles, music, and clothing. Owner H. H. Leonard opened the doors to the Mansion on Valentine's Day, 1980. The venue serves as a hotel, artist residence, venue for concerts and special events, and the O Museum focuses on arts and social justice.

One of the people featured in the museum is Rosa Parks (1913-2005), the "mother" of the Civil Rights Movement. Parks is known for her brave refusal to give up her seat to a white man on a public bus in Montgomery, Alabama in 1955. The event sparked the year-long Montgomery Bus Boycott. In 1994, at the age of 81, Parks was robbed and attacked in her home in Detroit, Michigan. Seeking a place to rest after this attack, Parks learned about Leonard and the Mansion's Heroes-in-Residence Program, which provides free rooms to people who serve others. Parks intended to spend a few days relaxing here, and she ended up staying here off and on for 10 years. Leonard and Parks became great friends, spending time in DC and traveling together.

Today, you can book a tour of the beautiful room that was Parks' home away from home, maintained in its original condition.

In 1999, President Bill Clinton awarded Parks the Congressional Gold Medal, the highest award bestowed by the US Government. This particular medal was designed by Artis Lane, a former Artist-in-Residence Program participant at the Mansion on O and longtime friend to Parks. The Black and Canadian artist also created the bronze bust of Parks that was installed in President Joe Biden's Oval Office, as well as the sculpture of abolitionist Sojourner Truth, the first such work in the US Capitol that honors a Black woman.

Address 2020 O Street NW, Washington, DC 20036, www.omuseum.org/touroperators |
Getting there Metro to Dupont Circle (Red Line); bus D6 to 20th Street & New Hampshire
Avenue NW, G2 to 20th & P Streets NW | Hours Tours Sun–Tue 9am–6pm, Wed–Sat
9am–9pm | Tip Snap a picture of the former home of Charles Hamilton Houston (1895–1950),
the renowned civil rights attorney who formulated the strategy leading to the US Supreme
Court's 1954 Brown v. Board of Education decision that racial segregation in public schools
is unconstitutional (1744 S Street NW).

63　Marion Barry Statue
Monument to the Mayor for Life

Marion S. Barry, Jr. (1936–2014) was elected to four terms as mayor of Washington, DC, and spent 16 years on the DC City Council. Barry is remembered as "Mayor for Life," a nickname that came about because of his ability to recover from personal and professional challenges and controversies. In 2018, an eight-foot-tall, bronze statue by artist Steven Weitzman was unveiled.

Barry was born in Mississippi, the son of sharecroppers. He moved to Tennessee and earned a bachelor's degree from LeMoyne-Owen College in Memphis, where he started becoming active in the Civil Rights Movement. He received his MS degree in organic chemistry from Fisk University, and he was elected as the first chairman of the Student Non-Violent Coordinating Committee (SNCC). He would move to Washington, DC in 1965 to establish SNCC in the capital.

Barry was elected to serve on the District's first school board, and then to the DC City Council. He was a formidable politician, known for building coalitions with marginalized populations. He founded Pride, Inc. in 1967 to employ young men who couldn't otherwise find work. More than 1,000 people enrolled that first summer. They had to commit to going to school and opening bank accounts at Black-owned Industrial Bank of Washington. This venture was the model for Barry's ongoing Summer Youth Employment Program. Barry kept the poor and elderly top of mind and made sure that there were recreation centers and pools for the city's youth.

In 1990, a misdemeanor drug conviction resulting from an FBI sting operation forced him to step down as mayor. Barry made a triumphant return to political office when he won back a seat on the City Council. In 1994, devoted supporters re-elected Barry as mayor in a landslide victory. Barry's constituents felt a sense of personal connection with him. He made a community feel taken care of as they had never been before.

Address 13½ Street & Pennsylvania Avenue NW, at the northeast corner of the John A. Wilson Building | Getting there Metro to Federal Triangle (Blue, Orange, Silver Lines); bus 32, 33, 36, 11Y, 16E, 52 to 14th Street & Pennsylvania Avenue NW | Hours Unrestricted | Tip Experience the Anacostia Riverwalk Trail by bike or foot while enjoying the Capitol Riverfront in DC. Download a trail guide, as well as a guide to the plants and animals of the Anacostia watershed (Navy Yard Metro, www.anacostiatrails.org).

64 Marianne's by DCCK

Stop in for lunch in Dr. King's honor

The Martin Luther King, Jr. Memorial Library was one of the first public buildings in the country named after Dr. King following his death. Designed to be a living tribute, the building hosts an exhibition space dedicated to telling stories about his impact locally. The library features artwork, local celebrity memorabilia, conference space, research libraries, and a multimedia exhibit about local civil rights leaders and important history.

There's another kind of living tribute to Dr. King in the lobby of the library: Marianne's by DC Central Kitchen (DCCK), a quick service café with light fare made from locally sourced ingredients. Like Dr. King, Marianne's is an advocate for people "facing high barriers to employment," according to their website. The friendly and conscientious staff at Marianne's has participated in DCCK's renowned training program, which has created opportunities for program graduates to work across Washington, DC's thriving culinary industry, including top restaurants, large hotels, corporate cafeterias, hospitals, schools, and other locations.

The café space is modern, bright and inviting with plenty of seating, and features light bites, snacks and beverages for breakfast and lunch. It is located on the ground floor, and it is the perfect place to have a cup of coffee, a delicious muffin, or a tasty hot sandwich. The menu changes regularly with new options for you to enjoy.

The café is named after Marianne Ali (1957–2017), a woman who overcame addiction and made a significant impact on the lives of more than 1,000 Washingtonians who came to DC Central Kitchen to realize their true potential. She was the long-time director of DCCK's Culinary Job Training program and received a White House Champions of Change Award and numerous other accolades for her transformative leadership and commitment to fostering dignity for all.

Address 901 G Street NW, Washington, DC 20001, +1 (202) 727-0321, www.dclibrary.org |
Getting there Metro to Gallery Place (Green, Red, Yellow Lines); bus X9 to 9th & G Streets NW,
or bus 80, P6, X2 to 9th & H Streets NW | Hours Mon – Thu 9:30am – 6pm, Fri & Sat
9:30am – 5pm | Tip Henry's Soul Food has been in operation since 1968, providing delicious
and affordable soul food, including their well-known sweet potato pies. They are also changing
lives through their Academy, which provides less affluent residents of Wards 7 and 8 with job
readiness opportunities (1704 U Street NW, www.henryssoulcafe.com).

65 Martin Luther King, Jr. Memorial

A closer look

The Martin Luther King, Jr. Memorial's address at 1964 Independence Avenue SW references the 1964 Civil Rights Act. It is the only memorial on the National Mall that honors an American who was Black and a civilian. In his *I Have A Dream* speech from the March on Washington for Jobs and Freedom on August 28, 1963, Dr. King stated, "With this faith we will be able to hew out of the mountain of despair a stone of hope." The monument depicts Dr. King carved into the Stone of Hope, with the Mountain of Despair behind him. From his 28-foot 6-inch high view, Dr. King gazes towards the horizon, concentrating on the future and his hopes for humanity.

James Simmons of the National Memorial Project Foundation revealed that upon close examination of the shrimp-pink granite used in the monument, you can see flecks of brown, black, white, and pink, a colorful mosaic mirroring the diversity of those who come to visit the memorial from around the globe. Third-generation stone carver Nicholas Benson created an original typeface called "King" to be used exclusively for this memorial in the quotes on the figure of King and along the north and south walls. When you enter the plaza from the street, look down to see the 10-inch medallion that covers a time capsule that is scheduled to be opened on August 28, 2061. Simmons explained that President Barack Obama, members of the King family, and special invitees placed items in the time capsule at the dedication.

Millions visit the Tidal Basin in springtime to view hundreds of cherry trees planted there, a gift of friendship to the United States from Japan in 1912. Additional trees were planted at the King Memorial as well. "The plaza comes alive each year during the blooming of the cherry blossoms, which is near the anniversary of Dr. King's death on April 4, 1968," says Simmons.

Address 1850 West Basin Drive SW, Washington, DC 20024, www.thememorialfoundation.org |
Getting there Metro to Smithsonian (Blue, Orange, Silver Lines); DC Circulator to Lincoln
Memorial (National Mall Line) | Hours Unrestricted | Tip On the north lawn of the
Department of Agriculture building, see a memorial marker at the base of a tree that was
dedicated to Dr. Martin Luther King, Jr. in 1983 (1400 Independence Avenue NW).

66 Mary Mcleod Bethune Council House

A pioneer in education and public service

Mary McLeod Bethune (1875–1955) was a passionate educator and an influential civil rights leader. She served as an advisor to four US presidents. Franklin D. Roosevelt appointed her Director of the Division of Negro Affairs for the National Youth Administration, making her the first Black woman to head a division of a Federal Agency. She was one of the women who helped lay the foundation for the modern Civil Rights Movement.

Bethune was born the 15th of 17 children in Maysville, South Carolina, the first of her siblings to be born free and to receive a formal education. In 1904, she established a school for girls in Florida, and in 1923, she negotiated the merger of her school with the all-male Cookman Institute, creating the four-year Bethune-Cookman College and becoming the first Black woman to lead a university.

In 1935, Bethune founded the National Council of Negro Women (NCNW), with a mission to lead, empower, and advocate for women of African descent, their families, and their communities. She purchased the Council House to use as her home and NCNW headquarters. A tour with a National Park Service ranger takes you through rooms on two floors, including her bedroom, which contains the walking stick given to her by FDR, and the dining room, the most important room in the house, where she held business meetings, board meetings, and strategy sessions and entertained dignitaries from around the world. Several period pictures document the people and work that took place here. One of the treasures in the house is a chandelier that formerly hung in the White House. The Council House includes the National Archives for Black Women's History and is the only archive solely dedicated to the collection, preservation, and interpretation of African American women.

Address 1318 Vermont Avenue NW, Washington, DC 20005, www.nps.gov | Getting there Bus 52, 54 to 14th & N Streets NW; DC Circulator to 14th Street & Rhode Island Avenue NW (Woodley Park-Adams Morgan-McPherson Square Line) | Hours Thu & Fri 9:30am–4:30pm | Tip The National Council of Negro Women raised the funds for the statue in Lincoln Park commemorating Mary McLeod Bethune, the first African American woman to be so honored in a public park in Washington, DC (1380 East Capitol Street SE).

67 Mary W. Jackson
NASA Headquarters
A brilliant scientist recognized

Mary Winston Jackson (1921–2005) excelled in academics in her high school in Hampton, Virginia, and went on to receive a degree in mathematics and physical science from the Hampton Institute. She eventually obtained work at the National Advisory Committee for Aeronautics (NACA), predecessor to NASA, in 1953 as a "human computer," a research mathematician who performed mathematical calculations by hand. She worked in a segregated division with other Black female mathematicians. Their work received national attention in the 2016 book *Hidden Figures* by Margot Lee Shetterly and the movie of the same name.

Jackson overcame barriers of segregation and gender bias to receive training for career advancement, and she was promoted to aerospace engineer in 1958. For Jackson, a love of science and a commitment to improving the lives of the people around her were one and the same. She once helped youngsters in a science club build their own wind tunnel. "We have to do something like this to get them interested in science," she is quoted as saying on the NASA website. "Sometimes they are not aware of the number of Black scientists, and don't even know of the career opportunities until it is too late."

In 2021, the NASA headquarters building was officially renamed after Jackson. Visit the Earth Information Center at Mary W. Jackson NASA Headquarters to see how the agency is collecting and analyzing data from its space satellites to help our own planet. You'll learn how the Earth is changing in six key areas: sea level rise and coastal impacts, health and air quality, wildfires, greenhouse gasses, sustainable energy, and agriculture. This information helps decision makers in developing the tools they need to mitigate, adapt, and respond to climate change.

Address 300 E Street SW, Washington, DC 20024, www.nasa.gov/headquarters/visiting-hq |
Getting there Metro to Federal Center SW (Blue, Orange, Silver Lines); bus P6 to 4th &
E Streets SW; DC Circulator to D & 7th Streets SW (Eastern Market-L'Enfant Plaza Line) |
Hours Mon–Fri 8:30am–5:30pm | Tip Built in 1886, Culture House was the home to the
Friendship Baptist Congregation for almost a century, and it was an integral meeting space for
the Southwest's Black community for decades. Today it provides a functional space for events,
exhibitions, workshops, and performances (700 Delaware Avenue SW, www.culturehousedc.org).

68 Maya Angelou Mural

Phenomenal woman, indeed

Marguerite Annie Johnson (1928–2014), better known as Maya Angelou, left an indelible mark on the world. Her many poems, books, quotes, and writings are filled with truth and inspiration for the ages. Angelou shared a treasure trove of wisdom that will never fade.

The beautiful and bright mural of Angelou is titled *Nourishing and Flourishing with Delight*. It was created by artist Eric B. Ricks, and it depicts Angelou with her eyes closed and her head tilted upwards. She is smiling brightly as if she is in a state of elation. Her hands are relaxed as if she has just released one of the birds depicted in the mural to fly off. Ricks says, "The main motif is a bird feeding a younger bird because she's nurturing the young mind."

Angelou's parents split up when she was very young, and she and her older brother, Bailey Jr., were sent to live with their father's mother, Anne Henderson, in Stamps, Arkansas, where, as a Black person, Angelou experienced firsthand racial prejudice and discrimination. She also experienced sexual abuse when her mother's boyfriend raped her during a visit. As vengeance for the sexual assault, Angelou's uncles allegedly killed the boyfriend. Angelou felt that her confession caused his death and was so traumatized that she didn't speak for years.

Angelou blossomed into a world-renowned poet, writer, singer, dancer, and actor. Most of her writings addressed racism, Black culture, and identity. Her autobiographical novel *I Know Why the Caged Bird Sings* (1970) was the first nonfiction bestseller by a Black woman and remained on the bestseller list for an unprecedented two years, selling over one million copies to date.

In 2011, President Barack Obama awarded Angelou the Presidential Medal of Freedom, the country's highest civilian honor. It was a fitting recognition for Angelou's remarkable and inspiring career in the arts.

Address 5600 East Capitol Street NE, Washington, DC 20019, www.muralsdcproject.com | Getting there Metro to Capitol Heights (Blue, Silver Lines); bus 96 to East Capitol Street & 57th Place NE | Hours Unrestricted | Tip Stop by the Deanwood Deli for creative sandwich options, including a John Wall ham sandwich, the Jive Turkey, and a Nannie Helen Burroughs Reuben. The deli is run by Capital City Restaurant Group, preserving our history while serving and enriching our communities (4505 Sheriff Road NE, www.capitalcityrestaurantgroup.com/deanwooddeli).

69 Meridian Hill/ Malcolm X Park

Follow the sound of the drums

Meridian Hill Park is a beautiful, 12-acre neighborhood park steeped in history. The name is based on the park's location on the longitude, or "meridian," of the District's original 1791 milestone marker. On his way out of office in 1829, President John Quincy Adams moved into a mansion built here. The park was later the site of a camp for Colonel Robert Gould Shaw and the 54th Massachusetts Union Army Regiment, the Northeast's first all-Black regiment. In the late 1800s, Meridian Hill hosted the Wayland Seminary and College for the education of formerly enslaved people.

At a 1969 rally, activist Angela Davis called for the park to be renamed after Malcolm X. Congressman Adam Clayton Powell introduced legislation to change the name formally, but it was unsuccessful. Nevertheless, the park was a hub of Black activism in DC for several decades, and many locals continue to call it Malcolm X Park.

The layout is a two-tiered design that features Italian Renaissance styling and landscaping. The upper tier is mostly grass, perfect for picnicking. The lower tier is concrete, designed as a formal garden with pools and statues. Staircases on either side of the park lead visitors between the tiers, while the water flowing between them is a 300-foot, 13-basin, cascading fountain, one of the longest in the country.

The park continues to serve as a gathering place for the community. An African drum circle has been meeting here on Sundays since the 1960s. The audience participates in storytelling, drumming, and dancing. The festivities take place during the warmer months beginning at about 5pm. At first, you may find just a few people with drums, but the circle can grow to about 20 drummers and as many dancers, as spectators swaying along to the beats. This is a family-friendly event mirroring the diversity in a city of young, old, rich, and poor.

Address 2500 16th Street NW, Washington, DC 20009, +1 (202) 354-6905, www.nps.gov |
Getting there Metro to U Street/African American Civil War Memorial/Cardozo (Green Line);
bus S2, S9 to 16th & Euclid Streets NW | Hours Daily, winter 6am–9pm, summer 6am–midnight |
Tip Oohhs & Aahhs Restaurant serves soul food favorites, like chicken, shrimp and fish for lunch
and dinner, along with brunch on weekends. The restaurant was featured on the "Diners, Drive-Ins,
and Dives," hosted by Chef Guy Fieri, and they gave a shout out to the wings and Cajun grilled
shrimp and grits (1005 U Street NW, www.oohhsnaahhs.com).

70 Mount Vernon
Remembering and honoring the unsung heroes

Mount Vernon is the estate home of George Washington (1732-1799), the first president of the United States. The success and wealth of the estate are directly tied to at least 577 enslaved people who worked here during Washington's lifetime.

The estate spans 500 acres and is now owned and maintained by the Mt. Vernon Ladies Association (MVLA). Your admission includes a guided tour of Washington's home, where you will learn about some of the enslaved persons who worked in the mansion. You can also tour the grounds and visit the recreated slave quarters for men and women and a cemetery of enslaved workers, which is recognized with a daily wreath laying. In 1929, a flat marker was added, followed by an upright memorial in 1983, designed by architecture students at Howard University. An ongoing archeological project to discover burial sites here has identified 70 of an estimated 155 graves.

Toiling as field hands, cooks, blacksmiths, or seamstresses, the workers here typically labored from sunrise to sunset – up to 14 hours during summer. Rohulamin Quander, author and retired senior administrative judge in DC, is a member of one of the oldest and consistently documented African American families in the nation. The family's 350-year history in Maryland and Virginia includes enslavement at Mount Vernon. Quander stated, "It is important for Americans to learn and understand that American history must reflect how enslaved men, women, and children, who received no compensation for their efforts, built not only Mount Vernon, but the basic early infrastructure of the nation's capital, including the US Capitol and the White House."

Join the "Enslaved People of Mount Vernon" tour, offered daily between February and December, and you will experience the estate through the eyes of Ona Judge, William Lee, and Hercules Posey, all once enslaved here at Mount Vernon.

Address 3200 Mount Vernon Memorial Highway, Alexandria, VA 22309, +1 (703) 780-2000, www.mountvernon.org | Getting there By car, take George Washington Memorial Highway to destination | Hours Daily 9am–5pm | Tip 1799 Prime is an award-winning restaurant owned by Jahmond Quander, specializing in steak and seafood for lunch, dinner and Sunday brunch. You'll also find a nine-panel mural commissioned for the restaurant that reflects key components of the Quander family's history (110 South Pitt Street, Alexandria, VA, www.1799prime.com).

71 Mt. Zion–FUBS Cemeteries

Uncovering Black Georgetown

Georgetown is the oldest community in Washington, DC, founded in 1751 along the Potomac River. Commerce thrived in the 1800s from the success of the tobacco industry and the slave trade. There were residences, shops, and schools in the growing community.

The Mount Zion Cemetery was formerly the Old Methodist Burying Ground, one of the oldest Methodist congregations in the world and known today as Dumbarton UMC. Black and white deceased parishioners were buried here. In 1816, 125 Black members, tired of the church's segregated policies, left to form the Mt. Zion United Methodist Church. The cemetery land was leased to Mt. Zion in 1879.

Some Dumbarton UMC members who were not supportive of the lease agreement had their white family members disinterred and reburied in the new nearby Oak Hill Cemetery, which was then racially restricted. The Female Union Band Society was a benevolent association made up of free Black women who bought the property adjacent to the Mt. Zion cemetery for the burial of freed Black people. Together, the two sections of land cover three acres.

According to Mt. Zion's death records, Black people in Georgetown worked as farmers, carpenters, carriage drivers, brick molder, hairdressers, housemaids, and over 100 other occupations. There are several people buried here who served in militias or in regular US Armed Forces. 6,313 burials here were recorded by the city's health office.

The cemeteries fell into disrepair for many years, and efforts are underway to preserve and restore the site. Some graves may never be found because they have sunk into the ground and hillsides, or because they are lost under vegetation. Located on the property is a vault used to store bodies temporarily prior to burial. The vault also served as a shelter for Black people escaping on the Underground Railroad.

Address 2501 Mill Road NW, Washington, DC 20007, +1 (202) 253-0435,
www.blackgeorgetown.com | Getting there Metro to Dupont Circle (Red Line); bus D2, D6
to Q & 27th Streets NW | Hours Unrestricted | Tip Pay homage at the site where the home
of Yarrow Mamout (1736–1823) once stood (now a private home). A devout Muslim all
his life, he went from being formerly enslaved to gaining his freedom and going on to become
a homeowner and Georgetown financier (3324 Dent Place NW).

72 National Air & Space Museum

Neal V. Loving's incredible folding plane

The collections of the Smithsonian National Air and Space Museum (NASM) were first housed in the ornate Arts and Industries Building, and it then expanded to a prefabricated building erected by the War Department and affectionately known as the bunker-like "Tin Shed." The collection opened to the public in 1920 and remained in use for the next 55 years. In 1946, President Harry S. Truman signed a bill establishing the museum as part of the Smithsonian Institution. Today, NASM is among the most visited museums in the world.

One of the key exhibits is the WR-3 airplane of Neal V. Loving (1916–1998), one of five planes that Loving designed and built. He flew the WR-3 for more than 690 hours and was the first Black American and the first person with double leg amputations to earn a racing pilot's license. Highly decorated, Loving had lost both legs in a glider crash in 1944, and he returned to flying by 1946. He co-founded an aircraft company, joined the Civil Air Patrol during World War II, and worked for the US Air Force at Wright Patterson Air Force Base near Dayton, Ohio, until he retired in 1982. The WR-3 has a very surprising but practical feature. Loving designed the wings to fold back, to allow him to tow the WR-3 behind his car and store the plane in his home garage. The plane's wingspan is 24 feet and 10 inches open and was only 94 inches when folded. When Loving was ready to fly, he simply unfolded the wings and locked them into place.

NASM maintains the world's largest collection of historic aircraft and spacecraft. It is undergoing a multi-year expansion and renovation, and the first phase opened in October of 2022 with eight new and renovated galleries. You can visit the planetarium and the museum store as well as the new Mars Café. The east wing of the museum will remain closed during renovations.

Address 6th Street & Independence Avenue SW, Washington, DC 20560, +1 (202) 633-2214, www.airandspace.si.edu | Getting there Metro to L'Enfant Plaza (Blue, Green, Orange, Yellow, Silver Lines); bus 32, 36, P6 to Independence Avenue & 6th Street SW; DC Circulator to Jefferson Drive & 7th Street SW (National Mall Line) | Hours Daily 10am–5:30pm | Tip Bronze is a restaurant inspired by Afrofuturism that melds fantasy and gastronomy with the culture of the African Diaspora. The upscale, three-level restaurant tells the imagined 700-year-old story of Alonzo Bronze, who traveled freely around the globe, searching for new cultures (1245 H Street NE, www.bronzedc.com).

73 National Museum of African Art

Wakanda forever!

In 1960, retired US Foreign Service officer Warren M. Robbins envisioned using African art to teach people about the continent, its people, and its cultures. In 1963, he established the Center for Cross Cultural Understanding to foster cross-cultural conversations about race to strengthen understanding and tolerance in communities. The center's first endeavor was to establish the nation's first museum of African Art in the Capitol Hill townhouse once owned by the great abolitionist and statesman Frederick Douglass. It would become part of the Smithsonian Institution in 1979.

Today, the museum showcases a rich diversity of artistic traditions from across the vast continent of Africa, through stunning and thought-provoking visual displays. You enter from the top, or Garden level. Exhibits are below on three sublevels, and each floor structured around a central, open atrium. The museum's cutting-edge performances and programs appeal to people of all ages.

The movie *Black Panther* broke box-office records when it was released in 2018, starring Chadwick Boseman as T'Challa, the king of the mythical and technologically advanced African nation of Wakanda. After the death of his father, T'Challa returns home to Wakanda to lead his people into the future. Marvel Studios knew the importance of getting the setting right and patterned some of the costumes and artifacts on objects from this museum. You can see some of these items in the permanent galleries, such as a red hat and multicolored, woven and beaded skirt made by a Zulu artist in South Africa.

And do not miss the museum shop because it offers a wide selection of merchandise inspired by the collections and the arts and cultures of Africa, including jewelry, clothing, handicrafts, books, music, and collectibles.

Address 950 Independence Avenue SW, Washington, DC 20560, +1 (202) 633-4600, www.africa.si.edu | Getting there Metro to Smithsonian (Blue, Orange, Silver Lines); bus 681, 881, 883, 884, 885, 886 to Independence Avenue & L'Enfant Plaza SW; DC Circulator to Jefferson Drive & 7th Streets SW (National Mall Line) | Hours Daily 10am–5:30pm | Tip A 10-foot-tall statue of Nelson Mandela, with his fist raised in a power salute, stands outside the South African Embassy. The image mirrors the photograph taken upon his release from prison after 27 years for opposing apartheid (3051 Massachusetts Avenue NW).

National Museum of Women in the Arts

Good hair or bad hair in Sonya Clark's Curls

The National Museum of Women in the Arts (NMWA) is the first major museum in the world solely dedicated to championing women through the arts. It reopened in October 2023 after a two-year, 70-million-dollar renovation. The museum's collections feature more than 6,000 works from the 16th century to today, created by more than 1,000 women artists from around the world, including Frida Kahlo, Rosa Bonheur, Lavinia Fontana, Amy Sharald, and Judy Chicago. There are five floors and the mezzanine to explore.

When you arrive at *Curls* by DC-native Sonya Clark, your first thought may be of several black party streamers cascading from ceiling to floor. As you move closer, though, you'll see that the "curls" are made up of hundreds of black hair combs. Clark is a textile and social-practice artist known for her mixed-media works that use simple objects, like beads, thread, and human hair to address complex themes of race and visibility, explore Blackness, and redress history.

Curls is a part of Clark's "The Comb Series." As she describes on her website, the work is concerned with "meaning in the materials." She states, "The black plastic combs evoke a legacy of hair culture, race politics, and antiquated notions of good hair and bad hair. What type of hair would easily pass through these fine-toothed combs? What does it mean that the combs themselves are arranged into tangles like felted dreadlocks, neat curls, and wavy strands?" Clark has seen her works of art exhibited in over 350 museums and galleries around the world.

The NMWA's gift shop sells only items sourced from businesses owned and operated by women. You'll find art, books, note cards, jewelry, scarves, and more, as well as items created by local artists and designers inspired by the museum's collection and exhibits.

1250 New York Avenue NW, Washington, DC 20005, +1 (202) 783-5000, www.nmwa.org   Metro to Metro Center (Blue, Orange, Red, Silver Lines); bus 3F, 3Y, 16G, 80, D6, G8, 68, X2 to H & 13th Streets NW   Tue–Sun 10am–5pm

The Washington Conservatory of Music & School of Expression operated in this building on T Street NW from 1903 until 1960 and was one of DC's earliest Black arts institutions. Harriet Gibbs-Marshall, the first Black person to graduate from the Oberlin Conservatory of Music, founded the school to inspire and train Black musicians and to preserve the rich heritage of Black music (902 T Street NW).

National Portrait Gallery

Black artists paint iconic Obama portraits

Since the administration of President George H. W. Bush, the National Portrait Gallery (NPG) has been commissioning portraits of American presidents in order to have an official likeness that is different from the presidents' official White House portraits. In 2006, starting with former Secretary of State Hillary Clinton, the gallery also began commissioning portraits of the first ladies. Former President Barack Obama's portrait was painted by New York-based artist Kehinde Wiley. Baltimore-based artist Amy Sherald painted former First Lady Michele Obama's portrait. They are the first Black artists to be commissioned to paint official portraits of a first couple for the NPG.

The visually stunning paintings of former President Barack Obama and First Lady Michelle Obama were placed on display at the (NPG) in 2018. Both portraits represent a notable departure from traditional representations of influential people, and they align with the Obamas' special interest in modern and contemporary American art. Wiley presents President Obama sitting forward in a wooden chair with his arms loosely crossed and exuding confidence. Behind him is a beautiful, leafy background with flowers that represent his heritage. Sherald depicts Michelle Obama elegantly seated, with one arm draped over her knee and the other arm bent upwards to support her chin, which rests on her hand. She is wearing a long and flowing sleeveless dress that reminded Sherald of a Gee's Bend quilt.

The president's portrait, on the second floor, is part of the nation's only complete collection of presidential portraits outside of the White House. You'll find the portrait of Mrs. Obama in a different gallery. From June 2021 to October 2022, the now-iconic paintings went on tour like rock stars to museums in Atlanta, Chicago, Houston, Los Angeles, and New York for millions of people to see.

8th & G Streets NW, Washington, DC 20001, www.npg.si.edu
Metro to Gallery Place (Red, Yellow, Green Lines); bus X9 to 9th & G Streets NW, 80, P6, X2
to 9th & H Streets NW   Sun – Sat 11:30am – 7pm   Visit the lobby of
the National Council of Negro Women, founded by Mary McLeod Bethune to view
historic displays in the only Black-owned building along historic Pennsylvania Avenue
(633 Pennsylvania Avenue NW, www.ncnw.org).

76 Ninety Ten by DC Sweet Potato Cake

Cooking with a conscience

April Richardson didn't plan to be a lawyer or to sell baked goods made with sweet potatoes. Nevertheless, she has now built successful careers out of both pursuits. The lawyer and business operations expert often volunteered her time to help turn struggling businesses around, and this is exactly what she did with DC Sweet Potato Cake.

Co-Founder Derek Lowery started a business with his mother Laurine's age-old family recipe for a sweet potato cake, a staple in Black cooking. Facing difficult times, the staff consulted with Richardson and later requested that she join their team. Under her leadership, the bakery grew from a small business to nationwide supplier. Their treats can be found all over the Washington, DC, Maryland, and Virginia area, including Wegmans, Starbucks, and Safeway. You can also buy them on QVC.

Ninety Ten by DC Sweet Potato Cake Bakery & Café opened in 2022 based on the idea that 90 percent of our diets should be healthy, and the remaining 10 percent can include guilt-free indulgences. The lovely and bright café with indoor and outdoor seating offers luscious baked goods alongside healthy options, including bowls, salads, and wraps. They also offer full-service catering and can create an entire menu consisting of sweet potato and non-sweet potato baked goods.

Cakes for the Cause is one of the café's initiatives that delivers "random acts of sweetness." During the 2020 pandemic, the team delivered over 5,000 treats to local hospitals for first responders and those working to serve the community. The company gave away 10,000 treats to local senior citizens in 2023 and hopes to double that in the future. Richardson also shares her business-building know-how at monthly events at the café for entrepreneurs.

Address 925 17th Street NW, Washington, DC 20006, +1 (202) 506-4457, www.dcsweetpotatocake.com, info@dcsweetpotatocake.com | Getting there Metro to Farragut West (Blue, Orange, Silver Lines); bus 38B, D6, G8, L2 to 17th & I Streets NW; DC Circulator to K Street & Connecticut Avenue NW (Georgetown-Union Station Line) | Hours Mon & Fri 8am–4pm, Tue–Thu 8am–5pm, Sat 11am–4pm | Tip Nearby Georgia Brown's restaurant has been serving up Southern hospitality alongside a rich and diverse menu featuring Low Country cuisine since 1993, including beloved Sunday brunch and live music (950 15th Street NW, www.gbrowns.com).

77 — Our Mother of Africa Chapel

A sacred space for reflection

There is a strong history of faith in Black communities that spans many religions. A beautiful representation of that faith can be found in the Our Mother of Africa Chapel at the Basilica of the National Shrine of the Immaculate Conception. Dedicated in 1997, the chapel was a gift from the National Black Catholic Congress under the leadership of the African American Bishops of the United States.

The pillars in the chapel represent the seven principles of African heritage, which include unity, self-determination, collective work and responsibility, family and cooperative economics, purpose, creativity, and faith. The chapel hosts walls of Botticini marble and a vaulted, mahogany ceiling. Fish and water symbols give the representation of being inside the hull of a ship. In fact, an inlay on the floor is an outline of the British merchant slave ship the *Henrietta Marie*, which sank off the coast of Key West in 1700 and was the oldest slave ship ever excavated.

Once inside the chapel, you'll be drawn to the sculpture of *Our Mother of Africa and Her Divine Son*, a depiction of Mary and the child Jesus. On the opposite side of the chapel is a six-foot-wide bas-relief of the African American story from slavery to emancipation. Both pieces were sculpted by Ed Dwight, former Air Force test pilot and the country's first Black astronaut candidate. Across the chapel, the crucified figure of Jesus was created by sculptor Juvenal Kaliki in accordance with the 500-year-old tradition of his Entabeni Tribe of Tanzania. The figure of Jesus hangs on a hand-oiled, cherry-wood cross created by artist Jeffrey Brosk. Visitors are welcome to the Basilica. You can take a self-guided tour, or you can register online for a guided tour. There's also a virtual tour of the chapel on the shrine's website.

Address 400 Michigan Avenue NE, Washington, DC 20017, +1 (202) 526-8300, www.nationalshrine.org, info@nationalshrine.org | Getting there Metro to Brookland-Catholic University (Red Line); bus H6 to Brookland-Catholic University | Hours Shrine April 1–Oct 1 7am–7pm, Nov 1–March 31 7am–6pm | Tip St. Augustine Catholic Church traces its heritage to 1858, seven years before the end of slavery in the country. It's frequently referred to as the "Mother Church" of Black Catholics and is open to all, with a focus on community (1419 V Street NW, www.staug-dc.org).

78 Paris Alexander Day Spa
Relaxing in-town getaway

The pleasant staff at Paris Alexander Day Spa have been pampering Washington's professionals for three decades. When you walk into the salon, you'll feel as if you've been invited into someone's home. The reception area is decorated in rich earth tones, while soft lighting highlights a brick wall and hardwood floors. Light music is playing, and a luxurious scent fills the air. You can enjoy a wide range of spa services here, including treatments such as the Parisian Classic, the Green Herbal Peel, massages, waxings, and many others. "We have the best facials in DC," says owner Paris Alexander.

Alexander grew up on a farm in South Carolina with her parents, sister, and brother. Her mother made all their clothing and taught Alexander how to sew. Her first passion was fashion, and she was also interested in education and teaching. Her father wanted her to attend trade school. "So the compromise was that I would do both at the same time," says Alexander. She attended a commercial sewing class at a local trade school while also attending college. After teaching for about a year, she came to visit her siblings in Washington, DC and decided to stay.

Alexander became a fashion coordinator at a local department store. She moved on to work at other establishments and separately attended classes that allowed her to learn and perfect new skills in makeup and skincare. "Everything sometimes is a matter of fate and being in the right place at the right time. I feel like that's been my journey," she says.

Upon a trip to New York to take a class in the late 1990s, an article about Black-owned spas in the well-known Black women's magazine *Essence* referred to Alexander. She called it the "Essence Rush," as she recounts. "I went from being a solo practitioner to very quickly hiring a staff because of the amount of business that article generated."

Address 1642 R Street NW, Suite 100, Washington, DC 20009, +1 (202) 466-8827, www.parisalexander.com, paris@parisalexander.com | Getting there Metro to Dupont Circle (Red Line); bus S2 to 16th & Corcoran Streets NW | Hours Sun 10am – 6pm, Mon, Wed – Fri 10am – 8pm, Tue noon – 8pm, Sat 9am – 6pm | Tip Nearby is the former home of Alain Locke (1886-1954), the nation's first Black Rhodes Scholar. He was also a central figure in the Harlem Renaissance (1326 R Street NW).

79 — The Pearl Incident

Largest attempted escape to freedom in US history

The Wharf is one of Washington, DC's newest trendy and fun destinations for locals and visitors alike, with a mix of restaurants, entertainment, and shopping. But as you stand here today, imagine that it's a rainy night in 1848, and 77 people, filled with a mixture of fear, hope, and determination are taking part in a plan to change the course of their lives by fleeing slavery. A small plaque located close to the water commemorates that fateful night.

DC was formerly a center for the slave trade in the United States, and while today it is busy and bustling, the Wharf neighborhood was secluded in 1848 and the perfect place to launch what would later be known as "The Pearl Incident," the largest recorded escape attempt by enslaved persons in American history. The organizers were free Blacks Daniel Bell and Samuel Edmonson. They secretly worked with abolitionists and other free Blacks to spread the word of the planned escape. Edward Sayres, captain of the 50-foot Schooner *The Pearl*, was hired to sail his vessel for this journey to freedom.

After dark on April 15, 1848, 77 enslaved men, women, and children silently boarded *The Pearl* and departed DC. Difficult weather conditions slowed their progress, and the ship eventually had to anchor near Point Lookout, Maryland. Time was not on their side.

When their enslavers realized that the escapees were gone, a group of outraged pursuers quickly organized and sailed down the Potomac River to capture the vessel the next morning. The freedom seekers were transported back to Washington and jailed. Several were sold to enslavers further south to work on cotton and tobacco plantations. Emily and Mary Edmonson, two of the children on board, were sold to enslavers from New Orleans, but their father was able to buy back their freedom. After their return, they became active in the abolitionist movement to end slavery.

Address Intersection of Pearl & Wharf Streets SW, Washington, DC 20024 | Getting there Metro to L'Enfant Plaza (Blue, Green, Yellow, Orange, Silver Lines) or Waterfront (Green Line); bus 52, 74, A8 to 7th Street & Maine Avenue SW | Hours Unrestricted | Tip The nearby Frederick Douglass Memorial Bridge honoring the great abolitionist opened in 2021, and you can walk or jog and enjoy pedestrian overlooks of the city and wharf (South Capitol Street SE, www.ddot.dc.gov).

80 Peterbug Shoe Academy
The king of E Street

John "Peter Bug" Matthews runs a shoe repair shop and an academy where young people can learn how to repair shoes and leather goods. Matthews also teaches them life skills, such as business skills, customer service, marketing, money management, and much more. He drives his Mobile Shoe Repair Lab to senior centers to provide his services at cost. He freely gives his time, money, and energy to help others. Mr. Peter Bug loves to say that his goal is "to save soles and heel people."

Matthews is a fifth-generation Washingtonian, who grew up in this Capitol Hill neighborhood. He faced many challenges in his youth, including a stammer when he talked, but with his mother's encouragement and help from teachers along the way, he worked hard to stay in school and follow a path that led him to becoming a skilled craftsman, a local leader, and an inspiration to many.

When you visit Matthews (and please call him Peter Bug), his door will be wide open. Or you'll find him sitting outside on Buchanon Plaza, in his kingly African attire, "holding court" for the steady stream of neighbors, visitors, and lifelong friends stopping by to say hello. Or they'll have shoes or bags in hand for a repair consultation. He can fix your red bottoms or your Birkenstocks, and it's clear he knows how to make things last. One of the tools that Matthews uses is a lasting machine created by Black inventor Jan Ernst Matzeliger (1852–1889) in 1883. It revolutionized the way shoes are produced even today. In 2022, the academy received status as a Historic Landmark in DC.

Each summer, hundreds of people from the DC area convene for food, music, dancing and games for the family as part of the official Peter Bug Day, aka BUGFEST. Matthews remains beloved by the community because he is constantly giving back. They even renamed his block of 13th Street where his shop sits "Peterbug Matthews Way."

Address 1320 Peterbug Matthews Way (E Street SE), Washington, DC 20003, +1 (202) 689-4549, www.Facebook.com, shoeshopboyz@gmail.com | Getting there Metro to Potomac Avenue (Blue, Orange, Silver Lines); bus 32, 36 to Pennsylvania Avenue & 13th Streets SE | Hours Tue – Fri 8am – 7pm, Sat 8am – 6pm | Tip John Harrod directed the longest surviving neighborhood arts center in DC from 1973 to 2008. The popular facility was a place for all types of artistic expression by aspiring youth and local and international artists. A plaque near this address commemorates his work (225 7th Street SE).

81 Provost

When you're here, you're family

A visit to Provost feels like a get-together with friends for great food and conversation. The restaurant fulfills a dream of owner Nina Gilchrist with a menu that's full of healthy, organic, and flavorful cuisine. "We place an emphasis on locally sourced and organic ingredients, authentic flavors, and a modern twist to classic dishes," says Gilchrist.

The sophisticated dishes include a popular red snapper, fried whole and served with coconut rice. Another favorite is Cajun chicken and shrimp pasta, made with tomatoes, spinach, and a Cajun cream sauce. The brunch menu includes traditional favorites, like avocado toast, chicken and waffles, and a variety of egg dishes.

The restaurant has a laid-back atmosphere that's warm, natural, and welcoming. You are greeted when you enter, and you can choose between sitting at the full-service bar or at one of the dining tables. A combination of neo soul and soulful pop music plays in the background. An eclectic mix of art and special pieces on display includes a work by author James Baldwin's sister, a bathroom with pictures that celebrate women, a quote from Khalil Gibran painted on the stairs between the first and second level, and a copy of a letter penned by Abraham Lincoln. The second level includes a large deck leading to a fully plant-based beer garden that will be open for dining and available to rent for special events during warmer months.

"We have several events on the weekend centered around community, art, and local entertainment," says Gilchrist. "Most events are free or offered at a nominal fee that goes directly to the artists." Remaining true to community connections, Provost hires local youth in the summer to give them real-life experience on a path that leads to culinary careers. Check the Provost website to see how you can view the reality docuseries that was produced about the restaurant, staff, and patrons!

Address 2129 Rhode Island Avenue NE, Washington, DC 20018, +1 (202) 200-9852, www.provostdc.com, connect@provostdc.com | Getting there Bus 83, 86 to Rhode Island Avenue & Thayer Streets NE | Hours Fri 5–10pm, Sat 10am–11pm, Sun 10am–10pm | Tip The Slowe-Burrill House in Brookland was owned by Lucy Slowe and her partner Mary Burrill. Slowe was the first Black woman to serve as dean of women at Howard University, and she was a founder of the Alpha Kappa Alpha sorority, the first sorority founded by Black women, among many other firsts (1256 Kearney Street NE, www.nps.gov/places/slowe-burrill-house.htm).

82 Queen City Sculpture
Reclaiming a lost community

Unveiled in June 2023, *Queen City* by artist Nekisha Durrett is a smokestack-like structure in Arlington's Metropolitan Park that pays homage to the thriving Black community that once existed on the site. Durrett commissioned 17 Black ceramicists to make the 903 teardrop vessels that hang within the 35-foot structure to represent the 903 people of Queen City, who were forced to leave their homes and their communities.

In 1863, the community of Freedman's Village was established on the property that is now Arlington National Cemetery to provide protection, education, and services to its Black residents, many of whom were once enslaved. The community thrived for several years, and although set up as a temporary refuge, residents fought to keep it open. The government closed the village in 1900, and residents were paid some compensation to vacate the area.

Many displaced residents relocated to East Arlington and an area that would become known as Queen City. After 40 years, this strong and unified community was also forced to close. The Federal Government exercised eminent domain to take over the land in 1942 for the Pentagon, giving residents a pittance and four to six weeks to leave. Moved by this story, Durrett formed a community of her own to produce *Queen City*, an important remembrance of a displaced community and the struggle of the families who lived there.

Durrett hopes that this work inspires and motivates people to make positive changes in their own communities. She explained in an interview with *The Guardian*, "This sculpture is almost mundane in its presentation. It was made using very humble materials, including 5,000 bricks similar to those from the area's former brickyards where many Black people found work. It looks like something from a bygone era, outdated infrastructure, like a well or a smokestack or something emerging from the ground."

Address 1400 South Eads Street, Arlington, VA 22202, www.nekishadurrett.com |
Getting there Metro to Pentagon City (Blue, Yellow Lines); bus 7A, 22A to South Eads &
13th Street South | Hours Daily dawn–dusk | Tip Nicole Fingers uses her love of art to craft
fine stationery at her boutique, Fingers in Ink. Fall in love with her ability to style and convey
your message brilliantly – and her Hello Kitty collection! (2642 North Pershing Drive,
Suite P4, Arlington, VA, www.fingersinink.com)

83 Rolloway Productions

Roll with a DC skating legend

If you fondly recall skating around a roller rink on classic skates, Rolloway Productions gives you the chance to relive that fun or to take classes and learn. Kenneth "Rollo" Davis, a professional quad skater for 40 years and an Apple-endorsed "skate legend," founded Rolloway Productions LLC in 2014.

"Rolloway Productions and Rolloway Skate University are special due to our inspirational founder, our approach to the role of roller skating in the community, and our transmission of the DC skate style and culture. We focus on community, family, and relationships," says Monica McNeal Boddie, Davis' business partner.

Davis played the lead character in the family-centric movie *Old School Rollers* (2021) about connecting generations, which was released to great reviews. In a book about his story, *The Life at the End of the Tunnel*, Davis shares how roller skating transformed him from living in addiction to becoming a beloved and inspirational contributor to the Black community.

McNeal Boddie says that roller skating is for everyone "from 3 to 73." When you arrive for a lesson, an initial assessment will ensure that you end up in the right class. If you're a beginner, you'll work on safety and stability while learning how to skate forward and backward, plus basic turns and transitions. You'll also learn how to fall and get back up safely. Intermediate skaters build on skate skills and discover their style through drills and other techniques. Advanced skaters take their talents to the next level with seasoned instruction and workshop opportunities, especially featuring Snapping, which is the skate style of Washington, DC.

Rolloway Productions host skating events with live DJs or specialty playlists, like gospel music. Skate rentals are available for a nominal fee, and skating is open to the public on designated days. You can also book the rink for private events.

Address Sk8Matrix, 3132 Branch Avenue, Temple Hills, MD 20746, www.instagram.com/ sk8matrix, www.facebook.com/rollowayproductionsllc | Getting there Metro to Naylor Road (Green Line); bus F14 to Naylor Road | Hours Classes: Sat 9:45 – 11:45am; check their social media for public skating hours and events | Tips The National Park Service oversees over 400 sites nationwide, and the Anacostia Skating Pavilion is the only skating rink in the system and the last one inside the District of Columbia (1500 Anacostia Drive SE, www.nps.gov).

84 Rose Park

The first African American sisters in tennis

Margaret and Matilda Roumania Peters were amongst the earliest Black tennis stars. From the late 1930s to the mid-1950s, sisters Margaret (1915–2004) and Matilda (1917–2003) exhibited exceptional skills at doubles play, earning them the affectionate nicknames of Pete and Re-Pete.

The Peters sisters played in the American Tennis Association (ATA), initially formed in 1916 to give Black athletes a chance to play competitive tennis at a national level during the era of segregation. The players were Black, but people of all backgrounds traveled to watch them play at ATA-sponsored tournaments around the country.

The Peters sisters began playing tennis as young girls at Rose Park, which was conveniently located across from their home on O Street in Northwest DC. They honed their skills through the years and were recruited to play at Tuskegee University on full scholarships. They won 14 doubles tennis titles, and their fame brought them audiences with celebrities and royalty. They even played tennis with Gene Kelly, who rented a house nearby. The Peters sisters were inducted into the Tuskegee University Hall of Fame in 1977.

The plot of land for Rose Park was donated in 1918 by the Ancient Order of the Sons and Daughters of Moses, an African American benevolent society, to give Black children in the neighborhood a nice place to play. The park was acquired by the city in 1922, and it became designated "For Coloreds Only." But both Black and white neighbors protested, and it continued to operate as one of the city's first integrated parks.

Today, it is a small, quiet park in Georgetown with a walking trail that passes nearby. The Friends of Rose Park website lists facilities including three tennis courts, a basketball court, a baseball diamond, two playground areas, a recreation center run by the DC Department of Parks and Recreation, and substantial open space.

Address 2600 O Street NW, Washington, DC 20007, www.roseparkdc.org | Getting there Metro to Dupont Circle (Red Line); bus G2 to 26th & P Streets NW | Hours Daily dawn–dusk | Tip Look for the historic marker that describes Herring Hill as a once thriving African American community. By 1776, a third of Georgetown's population was African American, as they worked in the many households and small businesses that arose by the 1860s (2701 P Street NW).

85 Rubell Museum DC

Historic schoolhouse becomes a work of art

If the goal of contemporary art is to challenge the status quo and reflect the times that we're living in, then the Rubell Museum succeeds on both counts. To begin, the execution of the renovation and remodel of its building challenges the norm. What was once the red-brick, historically Black Randall Junior High School is now combined with a sleek, modern entryway to create an updated and urban feel. Secondly, the art in the collections here is visually stunning and thought-provoking. You may even find that it can elicit unexpected emotion at times.

"The Rubell Museum features two dozen galleries where local DC residents and visitors can engage with contemporary artworks that address the most pressing social and political issues of our time, providing a springboard for learning and discourse," says Museum Director Caitlin Berry. "Visitors can explore artworks by some of the foremost contemporary artists working today, such as Rashid Johnson, Carrie Mae Weems, and Nina Chanel Abney, as well as artists local to the DMV area, like Sylvia Snowden and February James."

Shortly after Mera and Don Rubell married in 1964, they started visiting artists' studios and collecting art in New York. Their son Jason Rubell joined them in 1982 to continue building the collection, creating the exhibitions, and developing the Rubell's art venues in Washington, DC and Miami.

A groundbreaking traveling exhibit curated by the Rubells is titled, "30 Americans." It showcases the story of Black humanity over 200 years with works by some of the most significant African American artists of the last four decades, including Jean-Michel Basquiat, Mickalene Thomas, Kara Walker, Hank Willis Thomas, and Kehinde Wiley. If it is not on display in DC when you visit, consider purchasing the over-200-page coffee table book in the museum gift shop. Museum entry is free for DC residents with proof of address.

65 I Street SW, Washington, DC 20024, +1 (202) 964-8254, www.rubellmuseum.org/dc, infodc@rubellmuseum.org   Metro to Navy Yard (Green Line); bus P6 to I Street & Wesley Place SW; DC Circulator to M Street & Delaware Avenue SW (Eastern Market-L'Enfant Plaza Line)   Sun, Wed & Thu 11am–5pm, Fri & Sat 11am–6pm   Look for the historic marker that chronicles important points in the incredible life of Dr. Dorothy Height, President Emmerita of the National Council of Negro Women (700 7th Street SW, www.hmdb.org).

86 — Shiloh Baptist Church
Greeting visitors in song

"These brethren, who have been driven from their homes and scattered among strangers, long to be gathered into a church that they may worship God unitedly as they formerly did." These words were spoken by the Rev. William J. Walker in 1863, petitioning a council of churches to establish Shiloh Baptist Church. The founders were 21 formerly enslaved men and women who had fled Fredericksburg, Virginia under the protection of the Union Army during the turbulent American Civil War.

The church has a beautiful, two-level sanctuary with a 52-foot-high ceiling. It also hosts a 2,642-pipe organ built by Casavant Frères in 1969. A nine-panel, stained-glass window tells the story of African people and their journey from collective slavery to individual prosperity in the United States. The window features geometric patterns from the Ndebele people of Zimbabwe in southern Africa and multicolored hands representing the church's racial and ethnic diversity and the idea of unity.

Shiloh has served through the years as a voice for the community, and today, under the leadership of the Rev. Dr. Wallace Charles Smith, the church continues its outreach by working to feed and clothe the homeless and by supporting local Scout troops.

Shiloh has welcomed countless famous visitors, from W.E.B. Du Bois and Dr. Martin Luther King, Jr. to presidents Ronald Reagan, George H.W. Bush, William Clinton, and Barack Obama. But all Sunday visitors can expect a warm welcome. Thomas Dixon Tyler, Shiloh's minister of Worship, Evangelism, and Discipleship, sees to that with his original composition performed each Sunday that ends with, "We are glad you're here today." Each December, Tyler produces a performance of Handel's *Messiah* that is free and open to the public. As of 2023, the 160-year-old church has the only Black church choir that has performed it for 85 consecutive seasons.

Address 1500 9th Street NW, Washington, DC 20001, +1 (202) 232-4288, www.shilohbaptist.org, sbc@shilohbaptist.org | Getting there Metro to Shaw-Howard U (Green Line); bus G2, G8 to 9th & P Streets NW | Hours Service Sun 9:55am, Office Tue–Fri 8am–5pm | Tip Metropolitan Wesley African Methodist Episcopal Zion Church was founded in 1832 and served as a former stop on the Underground Railroad. It was also the location of the first public school for Black children in the city. Look for the marker that tells the story of this church (1712 North Capitol Street NW, www.metropolitanwesley.org).

87 Sio Ceramics

Handmade, wearable, and useful

Makeda Smith is inspired by color, pop art, nature, functionality, and simplicity. She brings these inspirations to life through Sio Ceramics, the business she founded in 2020. Smith hand-crafts wearable art pieces and household items that are also works of art. She belongs to a group of local ceramic artists and says that hers is the only Black- and woman-owned ceramics studio in the city of Washington, DC.

Smith has carved out a niche for herself among young artists in the region. When you visit her shop on any given weekend, you'll join a steady stream of customers shopping for gifts – or for themselves. "I would say that my business itself shows that there are many types of art forms that Black creatives can be interested in," Smith says. "You can be a Black artist that makes a living from their work."

Smith studied art as a minor in college. She calls her years as an art student "low key" because she was not confident in her work. "After a few years of teaching elementary school, I felt something was missing. My creative muscle had atrophied, and I felt unfulfilled," she says. After coming to this realization, Smith started to work with clay again, slowly building herself up. "I started with a home art show, where I put up all my art pieces and invited all my friends over to see my work."

Then Smith co-created and hosted an event called The Funktion. This experience was a personal turning point for her. "I made wearable art and jewelry. We executed a runway fashion show and art exhibition. This event forever changed how I saw myself. The title of 'artist' finally stuck," she recounts.

Smith stays connected to the local community by hosting cultural events and by offering pottery making classes. In the future, she would like to begin creating gallery pieces and transition into more of a fine art space. For now, her journey has not slowed, and she has never looked back.

Address 716 Monroe Street NE, Studio 11, Washington, DC 20017, +1 (202) 271-3253, www.sioceramics.com, sioceramicsdc@gmail.com | Getting there Metro to Brookland-CUA (Red Line); bus 80, G8, H6, H8, H9, R4 to Brookland-CUA | Hours Sat 10am–2pm | Tip Shop for soft, breathable, organic cotton products for children, from newborn to four years old, made with environmentally friendly, organic cotton fabrics and non-toxic inks at YiniBini Baby (716 Monroe Street NE, Studio 17, www.yinibinibaby.com).

88 The South Boundary Stone
Benjamin Banneker and the first federal monuments

Benjamin Banneker (1731-1806) learned to read from his maternal grandmother and spent a short time in a Quaker schoolhouse. A self-taught astronomer and mathematician, Banneker was born a free Black man in what is now Ellicott City, MD.

After the location of the new capital city was selected in 1790, President George Washington (1732–1799) hired surveyor Andrew Ellicott (1754–1820) in 1791 to plot the boundaries of the 100-square-mile area with a team that included Banneker. The boundary markers are roughly hewn stones that include the inscription "Jurisdiction of the United States," the milestone's number, the name of the border state–Virginia or Maryland–the year in which the marker was laid, and its compass reading. Today, nearly all 40 of the more than 200-year-old stones are visible with varying degrees of decay.

The South boundary stone was the first one laid using Banneker's calculations. You can find it today in the sea wall separating Jones Point Park from the Potomac River, land that Virginia took back from DC in the 1846 retrocession. The stone is underground and visible through a glass dome near the lighthouse. The park runs along the Potomac River and has recreational offerings that include a canoe launch, picnic areas, fishing piers, and walking and biking trails.

Banneker's additional accomplishments include carving a wooden clock that kept accurate time for decades until it was destroyed in a fire. He successfully forecasted a solar eclipse, and he published scientific almanacs. He also famously corresponded with Thomas Jefferson (1743–1826), challenging the then secretary of state on his hypocrisy in declaring all men equal in the Declaration of Independence while remaining a slave holder and fighting the British for independence. Abolitionists and civil rights activists often cited the brilliant work and scientific contributions of Banneker to support their calls to end slavery.

Address Jones Point Park, Woodrow Wilson Bridge, Alexandria, VA 22314 |
Getting there Bus 10B, 11Y to South Washington & Church Streets | **Hours** Daily 6am–10pm |
Tip Benjamin Banneker Park honors one of the most famous Black men in colonial America.
He was a farmer, mathematician, inventor, astronomer, writer, surveyor, scientist, and humanitarian
(429 L'Enfant Plaza SW, www.nps.gov).

89 The Spice Suite

Couture blends to elevate your kitchen

Angel Gregorio's website describes her as "Community Servant. Innovator. Philanthropist. Disruptor." It's a fitting description for one of DC's most recognized Black entrepreneurs, who went from working as an assistant principal to becoming the owner of a successful business in less than two months.

Gregorio is the founder of The Spice Suite, a boutique where you can find exotic and tantalizing gourmet spices, infused oils, and other culinary delights. Her couture blends and ensembles of spices and herbs inspire chefs and home cooks alike. The atmosphere is beautiful, hip, and welcoming.

You'll enjoy browsing the striking displays of bold and fashionably branded products, including glass jars of flavorings called Applewood Chipotle, For City Girls, Sweet Vanilla, and countless others. You can find the full collection of products in the store. The online shop offers themed boxes and bags with spices, blends, oils, and sauces.

Gregorio's idea for this venture was born when she walked past a building that was for lease and inquired about the rent. Instead of giving her a price, the owner asked her what she would do with the space. She had no idea, but upon his further inquiries, she told him that it would be a spice shop. And the rest is history.

After stocking her shelves with spices, she decided to offer empty space for free to small Black-owned businesses to sell their handmade products and has hosted more than 2,300 pop-up shops. In 2023 she also became owner of the city's first Black-owned shopping center, Black + Forth, offering affordable commercial space for Black business owners, along with education for the Black community in all aspects of entrepreneurship.

Gregorio is a DC native who also attended Howard University. She has a love of education and children, and she personally works to improve the lives of the city's most vulnerable youth and families.

Address 2201 Channing Street NE, Washington, DC 20018, +1 (202) 506-3436, www.thespicesuite.com, whatsup@thespicesuite.com Getting there Bus H6 to Franklin & 22nd Streets NE Hours Fri & Sat noon–6pm, Sun noon–5pm Tip Nearby Roaming Rooster expanded from one food truck to three and numerous brick and mortar locations where you can savor amazing and fresh fried chicken sandwiches made from free-range, grain-fed, and antibiotic free chicken (3176 Bladensburg Road NE, www.roamingroosterdc.com).

90 Spirit of Freedom Memorial

Lest we forget

The bronze Spirit of Freedom Memorial, also known as the African American Civil War Memorial, was dedicated on July 18, 1998 and serves as a tribute to the 209,145 United States Colored Troops (USCT), who helped bring an end to the institution of slavery and keep the United States under one flag.

The memorial designer and sculptor was Ed Hamilton of Louisville, Kentucky. "I found a wonderful book called *Colored Soldiers* by William Gladstone. He did a historical photo book on actual photos of soldiers back during the Civil War era. So that book allowed me to be able to see actuality from that time period," said Hamilton in an interview with the National Endowment for the Arts.

The memorial includes four eight-foot-tall figures, three soldiers holding rifles and one sailor holding a ship's wheel. On the other side of the memorial is a family with their son preparing to leave for war. Rarely noticed is a face that looks out over the soldier's heads from within the wavy surface of the 11-foot pylon in the center of the memorial. While contemplating the subject of his design, Hamilton thought about where one turns when facing danger on the battlefield. He created this face, which he called, "The Protector."

Connected granite walls surrounding the main sculpture list the names of all 209,145 heroic servicemen and officers on metal plaques. Included among those names are ancestors of former First Lady Michelle Obama: Jerry Sutton/Suter, 55th USCT (Wall C, plaque 67); and Caesar Cohen, 128th USCT (Wall D, plaque 134), who was her paternal great-great-grandfather.

Nearby is the African American Civil War Museum, which tells the stories of the USCT. It is housed in the historic Grimke School, one of the country's first schools for Blacks after the Civil War ended.

Address U Street & Vermont Avenue NW, Washington, DC 20001, +1 (202) 667-2667, www.afroamcivilwar.org, museum@afroamcivilwar.org | Getting there Metro to U Street/African American Civil War Memorial/Cardozo (Green Line); bus 63, 64, 90, 92, 96 to Vermont Avenue & U Street NW | Hours Unrestricted | Tip In the National Gallery of Art, the plaster cast of the Shaw 54th Regiment Memorial (1900) by Augustus Saint-Gaudens commemorates the valiant efforts of Colonel Robert Gould Shaw and the men of the 54th Massachusetts, the second Civil War regiment of African Americans enlisted in the North (6th Street & Constitution Avenue NW, www.nga.gov).

91 Studio Acting Conservatory
The Last Supper in Black

The Studio Acting Conservatory's (SAC) building exterior is hard to miss. The bright red building is a cross between a barn and a church that somehow fits right into the Columbia Heights neighborhood.

The space was formerly occupied by New Home Baptist Church, which relocated to Maryland. The property changed hands a time or two before it came under SAC's ownership, and the space required quite a bit of work by then. During renovations, the contractors discovered a buried treasure behind the drywall. It was an astonishing and massive bas-relief depicting the Last Supper with Jesus and the 12 disciples beautifully sculpted onto an entire wall.

Artist Akili Ron Anderson was the first chair of the Art Department at Duke Ellington School of the Arts in DC. In the early 1980s, prior to the church's move to Maryland, a deacon who was acquainted with Anderson asked him if he would create a mural for the church. Anderson, who is now an art professor at Howard University, agreed. But instead of a mural, he crafted the stunning artwork using faces that resembled the African American men he saw as a child in what was then a Black community. Anderson says that he grew up across the street and wanted his mother to see it and be proud of his work. She loved it. "With all the facilities of my mind and spirit, and by my hand, together with my community, my goal is to celebrate African American people and culture," Anderson states on his website.

Due to logistical issues, the church was sadly unable to take the work with them when they relocated, and it was eventually covered up and lost. Fortunately, you can make an appointment and go see it once again. Anderson's many other works include sculptures and stained glass windows for Howard University's Andrew Rankin Chapel and the Columbia Heights Metro station.

Address 3423 Holmead Place NW, Washington, DC 20010, +1 (202) 232-0714, www.studioactingconservatory.org, info@studioactingconservatory.org | Getting there Metro to Columbia Heights (Green, Yellow Lines); bus 52, 54 to 14th & Newton Streets NW | Hours See website for schedule | Tip Grab a sweet treat at Here's The Scoop premium ice cream and dessert shop where their motto is "Bringing the community together one treat at a time" (2824 Georgia Avenue NW, www.heresthescoopdc.com).

92___Sweat DC
Church for weights

Sweat DC is a fitness studio where you can walk in with confidence, even if you've never lifted a weight in your life. Owner Gerard Burley, also known as "Coach G," has a master's degree in sports and exercise and once played professional basketball in Italy. Burley believes that fitness should be fun, and so he founded Sweat based on a strong principle: Come as you are. He aims to encourage and inspire people to become better versions of themselves from the inside out through hard work and determination.

Burley and his team of coaches know that walking into a gym can be intimidating. "I grew up as a gay, Black boy in West Baltimore, so I know what it feels like to not feel included in the world," says Burley. "And I also know what it feels like to feel empowered through fitness." He always had an interest in sports, but at the age of 18, his mother passed away, and he turned to fitness to channel his emotions and help him deal with the tremendous loss. "Sometimes when we face hardship, we find different meanings in different sanctuaries," says Burley. He sometimes refers to Sweat DC as "church for weights."

The one-room studio is filled with weights, mats, and equipment. During the coach-led classes, the lights are low, and colored lighting creates a nightclub feel, while a variety of musical genres play over the sound system. Videos with people demonstrating proper form play on monitors hung high on the walls. The visuals help everyone to stay mindful, and so anyone who is hard of hearing can watch the videos and feel the vibration of the music. "It's strength-based, group personal training," says Burley. "The workouts are not random. They're based on a science-backed program that changes each month, and we are looking at how you get better each month." Burley wants students to have a fun, challenging and empowering experience, and he looks forward to expanding the business.

Address 3325 Georgia Avenue NW, Washington, DC 20010, +1 (202) 780-5286, www.sweatdc.com, info@sweatdc.com | Getting there Metro to Georgia Avenue-Petworth (Green Line); bus 70 to Georgia Avenue & Lamont Street NW | Hours Mon–Fri 6am–7pm, Sat & Sun 8:30am–11:30am | Tip Sidebarre is a high intensity, low impact, full-body workout to build and tone in DC. No dance experience is required, but all instructors are technically trained in ballet and fully aware of how the body moves (3400 14th Street NW, www.sidebarredc.com).

93　Sycamore & Oak
Promoting Black business

The Retail Village at Sycamore & Oak opened in Congress Heights in 2023. This architecturally stunning, timber, commercial building houses local Black-owned businesses and space for events. This venue is the result of a partnership between developers and existing residents to ensure that those who live here will benefit as the area changes. The current, 22,000-square-foot structure is part of a larger, five-acre development that will bring affordable housing and the first full-service hotel east of the Anacostia River once the project is completed.

The anchor store here is The Museum, founded by LeGreg Harrison, a key collaborator in envisioning Sycamore & Oak, and partner Muhammed Hill, both DC natives. Harrison describes The Museum as a "fashion art gallery." It brings together a passion for art which he realized he had at an early age, and sports, as both Harrison and Hill were celebrated athletes in their youth. They're also tied to the music business, having worked on the management team of multi-platinum, DC-born rapper Wale.

The Museum's brand itself features a colorful mix of bold typography and graphics placed creatively on everything from hats and shirts to jackets and footwear. "We wanted to make sure people had a place where they could come and see the trendy street fashions that were started in DC as far back as 1979," says Harrison. In 2022, The Museum became the first Black business to design guest services wear for an NFL franchise, the Washington Commanders.

Everything they do connects with the community. "We understand that the way we keep getting is to keep giving," says Harrison. They launched a non-profit organization called Future Moguls, to help kids aged 12 – 18 discover their potential as entrepreneurs. They've also partnered with David Yurman jewelry and basketball legend Stephen Curry for events that give back to the community.

Address 1110 Oak Drive SE, Washington, DC 20032, www.sycamoreandoak.com
Getting there Metro to Congress Heights (Green Line); bus W1, W2, W3, W4 to
Alabama Avenue & 12 Street SE Hours Tue–Thu 11am–7pm, Fri & Sat 10am–8pm,
Sun noon–5pm Tip The Escape Allée at the Douglas Community Center commemorates
the path from enslavement Frederick Douglass took on September 3, 1838. He traveled
by train, ferry, and steamboat through Maryland, Delaware, Pennsylvania, and New York.
Each tree here represents one of these four states (1922 Frederick Douglass Court SE).

94 Terrell Place

A champion for change

You've probably passed Terrell Place many times, and you may even remember shopping in this building. The name Terrell Place doesn't stand out like the nearby Capital One Arena or the Shakespeare Theater, but this ordinary building holds an extraordinary place in history. It is named in honor of Mary Eliza Church Terrell (1863-1954), influential educator and activist for civil rights and women's suffrage.

Terrell was born Mary Eliza Church in Memphis, Tennessee to formerly enslaved parents. She embraced their belief in education and hard work. She attended Oberlin College, where she became one of the first Black women to earn a college degree. She would also earn her master's degree in education. After marrying Robert Heberton Terrell in 1891, she moved with him to DC, where he would become the city's first Black municipal judge.

Terrell focused on securing the right for women to vote. She encountered reluctance from the leaders of that movement to include Black women in their efforts, and she fought to change those conditions. She spoke out frequently about the issue and then co-founded the National Association of Colored Women in 1896. She became a charter member of the National Association for the Advancement of Colored People (NAACP). She was the first Black woman ever appointed to a school board.

The building is the former Hecht Company department store, once a popular shopping destination. During the era of segregation, Hecht's was open to all, but the cafeteria was segregated. An NAACP committee chaired by Terrell participated in organized boycotts, picket lines, and sit-ins throughout DC. They convinced over 40 restaurants, including Hecht's lunch counter, to stop discriminating.

A plaque commemorating her life wraps the corner of the building and includes an engraved image of Terrell. A nearby marker on the corner provides more of the history.

MARY CHURCH TERRELL

Terrell Place is named after
Mary Church Terrell (1863-1954)
Teacher, Writer, Civil Rights Activist

Mary Church Terrell championed equal
rights throughout her life — locally, nationally,
and internationally.

Address 7th & F Streets NW, Washington, DC 20004 | Getting there Metro to Gallery
Place-Chinatown (Green, Red, Yellow Lines); bus 70, 74 to 7th & F Street NW | Hours
Unrestricted | Tip You can see the exterior of the unique half-house in LeDroit Park where
Mary Church Terrell and her husband lived (326 T Street NW, www.nps.gov).

95 Theodore Roosevelt Island

Natural paradise with a story to tell

You may be familiar with Roosevelt Island if you regularly run, hike, or bike through the Potomac Heritage Trail or other interconnected trails. If not, you will want to visit this peaceful and scenic island to pay homage to those who once lived here.

The island is on the Potomac River, not far from Arlington National Cemetery in Virginia and Georgetown in DC. It was dedicated in 1967 in honor of 26th President Theodore Roosevelt to commemorate his conservation efforts. According to the National Park Service website, he placed almost 230 million acres of land under the protection of the Federal Government. Look for the memorial plaza and the 17-foot statue of the president.

The island's first inhabitants were the Nacotchtank Indians, who lived, hunted, and traded here on what they called Analostan Island. The Nacotchtank were also known as the Anacostian, Anaquashtank, and Nacostine, the origin of the name of the Anacostia community in DC. Colonists displaced the Native Americans in the late 1600s, and the island's ownership changed hands many times before it became a residence and mustering point in 1863 for the 1st US Colored Troops, Black men who volunteered to fight for the Union Army in the American Civil War. During the last year of the war, the island was a Freedman's village for formerly enslaved people.

The island comprises 88.5 acres and has three walking trails and a memorial plaza. The Swamp Trail is a 1.5-mile loop that passes through woods and marshland. It is part gravel and part boardwalk. The .3-mile Woods Trail takes you past the memorial plaza. The .75-mile Upland Trail traverses the length of the island. Every Saturday between May and October, you can join the National Park Service for a walking tour of the Island to learn about its history and former owners and inhabitants. Please note that bikes are not allowed on the island.

Address George Washington Memorial Parkway, Washington, DC 22211, +1 (703) 289-2500, www.nps.gov | Getting there Metro to Rosslyn (Blue, Orange, Silver Lines); bus Arlington Transit 55 to Langston Boulevard & Nash Street. Take the Custis Trail to the Mount Vernon Trail to the footbridge onto the island. | Hours Daily 6am–10pm | Tip The Contrabands and Freedmen Cemetery served as the burial place for about 1,800 Black people who fled to Alexandria to escape from bondage during the Civil War. A memorial was opened in 2014 on the site of the cemetery to honor the memory of the Freedmen, the hardships they faced, and their contributions to Alexandria (1001 South Washington Street, Alexandria, VA, www.alexandriava.gov).

96 Thurgood Marshall Center

A tale of two heroes

The Thurgood Marshall Center for Service and Heritage/Anthony Bowen YMCA pays homage to two heroes in Black history. Thurgood Marshall (1908–1993) was a civil rights lawyer and the first Black US Supreme Court justice. He fought against segregation and argued the historic 1954 *Brown v. Board of Education* case, in which the Supreme Court declared that it was unconstitutional to separate children in public schools based solely on their races.

The Reverend Anthony Bowen (1809–1871) fought for a better life for Black families and founded the first Young Men's Christian Association (YMCA) in 1853. Bowen, formerly enslaved on a Maryland plantation, purchased his freedom for $425 and later the freedom of his wife. He moved to Washington, DC, where he organized a church, a school, and the YMCA, which was, at first, a club that met at his home on E Street SW on Sunday afternoons.

The building served as a YMCA until 1982. Today, it is home to a small museum. It also hosts community programs and events and provides office space for organizations that serve the community. Upon entering there is a display entitled *Pullman Porter Memories* commemorating the African Americans who worked on Pullman railroad cars from 1868-1968 including a dining menu, china, and a Pullman stock certificate from 1925. A museum room represents a typical residential home in the U street/Shaw neighborhood between 1910 and 1950. Walk around the meeting rooms and gymnasium to see walls adorned with historic photos and concert flyers with artists like Aretha Franklin, Little Richard, and Otis Redding, along with people participating in activities in the building. The *Precious Memories Dorm Room* is the last of the original 54 dorm rooms that were used for stays by students and professors from Howard University and visitors including Thurgood Marshall, Langston Hughes, and soldiers during wartime.

Address 1816 12th Street NW, Washington, DC 20009, +1 (202) 462-8314, www.tmcsh.org | Getting there Metro to U Street/African American Civil War Memorial/Cardozo (Green, Yellow Lines); bus 63, 64 to 11th & S Streets NW, or bus 52, 54 to 14th & T Streets NW | Hours Mon–Thu 9am–5pm, Fri 9am–2pm | Tip "America's diversity offers so much richness and opportunity. Take a chance, won't you? Knock down the fences, which divide. Tear apart the walls that imprison you. Reach out. Freedom lies just on the other side. We shall have liberty for all." – Thurgood Marshall. Listed on a callbox near to where he lived briefly (57 G Street SW).

97 — Torpedo Factory Art Center

Art for everyone

A fun day at the Alexandria Waterfront should include a visit to the Torpedo Factory Art Center (TFAC). Like many area buildings, the TFAC is steeped in history. Construction began in 1918 at the end of World War I, and the facility was used for the manufacture and maintenance of Mark III torpedoes, similar to the one you will see at the Riverfront entrance. There is also a Mark XIV torpedo used in World War II on display. Black men and women found an increasing number of job opportunities at facilities like this after President Franklin Delano Roosevelt desegregated the defense industries in 1941.

In 1974, the City of Alexandria cleaned out the old government building complex to create a working space for artists, designating it the Torpedo Factory Art Center. As noted on their website, the TFAC values a diverse community of artists and staff that reflects representation from different social, economic, and cultural backgrounds, as well as different artistic media, styles, and forms of expression. The Art Center values artists of all stages of their career, regardless of their formal arts training.

The building has the look and feel of a modern warehouse with three levels, where you can wander among more than 150 artists' studios, seven galleries, The Art League School, and the Alexandria Archaeology Museum. Even if you don't consider yourself an art lover, you'll probably find something here that piques your interest. Chat with artists as they work, and browse and purchase a variety of art forms including oil painting, jewelry, metalwork, ceramics, and much more.

Visit the Alexandria Archaeology Museum to view maritime and city-specific exhibits. The Art League School offers courses in a variety of media, where you can learn anything from making comics or painting with watercolor to photography or producing stained glass panels.

Address 105 N Union Street, Alexandria, VA 22314, +1 (703) 746-4570, www.torpedofactory.org, torpedofactory@alexandriava.gov | Getting there Metro to King Street (Blue, Yellow Lines); DASH bus 30, 31, 34 to North Fairfax & King Streets | Hours Daily 10am–6pm | Tip African American Heritage Park was created on the site of the city's oldest known independent African American burial ground, the 19th-century Black Baptist Cemetery. Visit the park's bronzed sculpture *Truths that Rise from the Roots – Remembered*, created by Jerome Meadows, which honors the contributions of Black people to the growth of Alexandria (500 Holland Lane, Alexandria, VA, www.alexandria.com).

98 Unique & Special Kids Spa
For mommy, daddy and mini-me

Unique and Special Kids Spa is true to its name. Children ages 3–16 can spend an afternoon being pampered in a place that has been designed especially for them. Owner Martia Clark has been a Virginia-licensed childcare professional for the past 20 years, working in early child development with a particular interest in the social and emotional well-being of children. In opening the spa, Clark created a place that gives children a space where they can relax and feel special.

The building that houses the spa is nondescript, but when you enter the spa, you will experience the wonder of a child. The reception area is quite colorful, and there are positive messages painted on the walls throughout the space. The spa offers typical salon services, such as manicures, pedicures, and facials for children and adults as well. You can upgrade the treatments so that Mom or Dad can enjoy the experience together with their kids. Younger children will love sitting in the child-sized treatment chairs and putting on comfy robes and slippers.

Turn up the volume for the kids by booking a fun and educational class or a full-blown party for about 10 children in the decorated party rooms. One room is filled with tents where kids can have a pajama party. Another is set with a red-carpet runway for princess or rockstar parties.

Kids can also take classes here, such as Cooking with Princess Tiana, where they learn to make a personal pizza or cupcakes. S.T.E.A.M. classes (science, technology, engineering, art, and math) provide a fun chemistry lesson combined with a spa experience. Dressed in lab coats, children will learn how to make a sugar scrub, bath salts, soap, or a similar product, while learning about the components and why they are beneficial.

Pick up some fun merchandise here too, including tutus to flip flops, if you don't want the experience to end.

Address 6911 Richmond Highway, Suite 405, Alexandria, VA 22306, +1 (703) 360-3700, www.uskidsspa.com, info@uskidsspa.com | Getting there Bus Fairfax Connector 151, 171 to Richmond Highway & Groveton Street | Hours Mon 11am–7pm, Wed–Sat 11am–7pm, Sun noon–6pm | Tip For great home-cooked southern cuisine like Mama used to make along with southern hospitality, visit nearby family-owned Della J's restaurant, open daily for lunch and dinner (7692 Richmond Highway, www.dellajs.com).

99 US Air Force Memorial
The Tuskegee Airmen fought for the nation

The United States Air Force (USAF) Memorial was dedicated in 2006 and honors all the men and women who have served in the USAF and its predecessors. The central part of the memorial includes three stainless steel spires that range from 201 to 270 feet high, evoking an image of jet and space vehicle flight. A USAF "star" seen on aircraft, missiles, and enlisted uniforms is embedded beneath the spires. Also on display is an eight-foot-high, four-person, bronze Honor Guard and inscription walls with the values of the Air Force.

One group that earned a special place in USAF history is the Tuskegee Airmen. They were the nation's first Black military pilots, who, despite obstacles from those who opposed integration, would set exemplary records during World War II and pave the way for desegregation in the military. Under increasing pressure from the NAACP, the Black press, and voters, President Franklin Delano Roosevelt opened the Civilian Pilot Training Program to Black trainees. Congress had created this program in 1939 to ensure that pilots would be available should war break out.

Nearly 1,000 pilots were trained at the Tuskegee Institute (now University) in Alabama. Serving in racially segregated units, the Airmen's success in escorting bombers during World War II is legendary. They had one of the lowest loss records of all the escort fighter groups, a record still unmatched, and they were in constant demand by allied bomber units for their services. They received several awards for their bravery and skills and have been memorialized in countless books, movies, and articles. Their stories also helped advance the American Civil Rights Movement.

The East Coast Chapter of Tuskegee Airmen, Inc. celebrates their legacy each year on the fourth Thursday in March with a wreath laying ceremony at the USAF Memorial. This event is free and open to the public.

Address 1 Air Force Memorial Drive, Arlington, VA 22204, www.afdw.af.mil/afmemorial Getting there Metro to Pentagon or Pentagon City (Blue, Yellow Lines); bus 16A, 16C, 16E, 16M to Southgate Road & Air Force Memorial Drive Hours Unrestricted Tip Columbia Air Center was the first Black-owned and operated airfield in Maryland, if not the nation, licensed in 1941 and in operation until 1956 and was used by Tuskegee Airmen (16901 Croom Airport Road, Upper Marlboro, MD, www.experienceprincegeorges.com).

100 US Capitol Building

Constructing freedom

Enslaved labor was used to construct many of the buildings in the new federal city in the late 1700s and early 1800s, including the US Capitol Building and the White House itself. The entire contribution of these laborers is unknown, but there is enough documentation to confirm the considerable work performed by enslaved people.

One of the most famous contributions at the US Capitol is that of Philip Reid (1820–1892). Reid was born into slavery in Charleston, SC and was purchased by Clark Mills to work in his foundry located in Bladensburg, MD. Although Reid was unable to read or write, Mills recognized his ironworking skills and included him on his team. Mills was selected to create the *Statue of Freedom* that stands today on top of the Capitol dome at 19.6 feet tall and weighing just under 15,000 pounds. At a point in the project, there was a contract dispute with a sculptor, whose demand for more money was denied. Reid was able to step up and figure out how to complete the complicated casting of the enormous statue.

Reid received his freedom on April 16, 1862, when President Lincoln signed the Compensated Emancipation Act. He was therefore a free man when the last piece of the *Statue of Freedom* was put into place on December 2, 1863.

Congress named the main area in the Capitol Visitors Center "Emancipation Hall" in 2007 to recognize the contributions of enslaved workers. In 2012, a marker and commemorative plaque were installed. They include a single block of Aquia Creek sandstone, which was originally part of the Capitol's east front portico. The original chisel marks on the sandstone are clearly visible so visitors can see the physical effort required to hew the stone. Also on display is a full-sized plaster model of the *Statue of Freedom*, an exact replica of the bronze statue on top of the Capitol dome. Take one of the daily tours offered, including "Heroes of Civil Rights."

Address First Street and East Capitol Street, Washington, DC 20510, +1 (202) 226-8000, www.visitthecapitol.gov | Getting there Metro to Capitol South (Blue, Orange, Silver Lines) or Union (Red Line); bus 32, 26 to First Street & Independence Avenue NE | Hours Mon – Sat 8:30am – 4:30pm | Tip Seek out the marker on the spot where orator, publisher, and statesman Frederick Douglass lived (316 A Street NE, www.hmdb.org).

101 US National Arboretum

An unexpected treasure

If you've even noticed the nondescript "US National Arboretum" sign and looked beyond the fencing along New York Avenue in Northeast, you've hopefully stopped to stroll through this peaceful retreat that spans almost 500 acres on Mount Hamilton.

The arboretum was established in 1927 within the US Department of Agriculture by an act of Congress, and it is a major institute for botanical research. People come here to meditate, walk, jog, picnic, take educational classes, or participate in events, including concerts, forest bathing walks, and yoga.

The land was converted from farmland and forest in the 1930s and early 1940s by hundreds of young Black men from DC, who were part of the Civilian Conservation Corps (CCC), according to Friends of the National Arboretum. The CCC was a New Deal-era program set up by President Roosevelt to combat unemployment among young men during the Great Depression. Over the nine years it existed, more than 3,000,000 American men planted more than three billion trees and constructed trails and shelters in more than 800 parks. They helped shape the modern national and state park systems.

Spring is the best time to experience the Azalea Collections to see thousands of azaleas in a blaze of color. There are several gardens and collections to enjoy all year, including the Friendship Garden of perennials, the National Bonsai & Penjing Museum of artistic trees and meditative gardens, and the National Grove of State Trees with specimens representing every state and the District of Columbia on a 30-acre parcel of land.

An unexpected treasure here is a set of 22 Corinthian columns that once stood at the United States Capitol building from 1828 to 1958. They were removed from the Capitol, as they didn't properly support the dome that would be built years later. The foundation on which the columns sit is constructed from steps originally at the Capitol.

Address 3501 New York Avenue NE, Washington, DC 20002, +1 (202) 245-4523,
www.usna.usda.gov | Getting there Bus B2, S41 to Bladensburg Road & Rand Place NE |
Hours Daily 8am–5pm | Tip The Cajun and Creole restaurant Po Boy Jim is a family-owned
business that brings New Orleans to DC (709 H Street NE, www. poboyjim.com).

US Supreme Court

First Black woman on the nation's highest court

"The judicial power of the United States shall be vested in one Supreme Court," begins Article 3, Section 1 of the United States Constitution, which was adopted in 1787 by delegates to the Constitutional Convention in Philadelphia. The first Supreme Court was made up of six white, male justices and was later expanded to seat nine justices. The court is slowly becoming more diverse and a better reflection of the people it serves.

On June 30, 2022, Justice Ketanji Brown Jackson was sworn in as a Supreme Court justice, the very first Black woman to serve on the highest court in the land. According to her Supreme Court biography, Jackson was born in Washington, DC and is married with two children. She received an AB from Harvard-Radcliffe College in 1992, and a JD from Harvard Law School in 1996. After working several years in the legal profession, in 2012 President Barack Obama nominated her to the US District Court for the District of Columbia, where she served from 2013 to 2021. President Joseph R. Biden, Jr. appointed her to the United States Court of Appeals for the District of Columbia Circuit in 2021 and then nominated her as an Associate Justice of the Supreme Court in 2022.

After her swearing in ceremony, Jackson said in a statement, "With a full heart, I accept the solemn responsibility of supporting and defending the Constitution of the United States and administering justice without fear or favor, so help me God. I am truly grateful to be part of the promise of our great Nation…"

Visit the Supreme Court to see the official portraits of Justice Jackson and the current Supreme Court Justices in the main reception area. Also look for portraits of past justices, including other justices of color Thurgood Marshall, Sonia Sotomayor, and Clarence Thomas, and special exhibits. The public can see the court in session on a first-come, first-seated basis.

1 First Street NE, Washington, DC 20543, +1 (202) 479-3000, www.supremecourt.gov/visiting/visiting.aspx   Metro to Capitol South (Blue, Orange, Silver Lines) or Union (Red Line); bus 32, 26 to First Street & Independence Avenue NE   Mon – Fri 9am – 4:30pm   Enjoy the colorful mural of a smiling Justice Ketanji Brown Jackson by artist Nia Keturah Calhoun. It represents the East Coast of America and the West Coast of Africa – and going from segregation to the Supreme Court in one generation – along with the glass ceiling Jackson had to break (1738 14th Street NW).

103 Visionaries of the Creative Arts

Living without limits

Taking in a performance by Visionaries of the Creative Arts (VOCA) should be on everyone's bucket list. Artistic Director Michelle Banks and Managing Director Nayte Paxton co-founded VOCA in 2019 in response to the need for a creative outlet for artists who are deaf or hard-of-hearing and BIPOC (Black, Indigenous, and People of Color).

After Banks directed Gallaudet University's Spring 2018 production of *A Raisin in the Sun*, she realized she had tapped into an incredible talent base among deaf people in the Black community. "The talent base that sprung up for an all-Black, deaf cast for *A Raisin in the Sun* needed more than just a 'one and done,'" says Banks. "These artists and so many other deaf BIPOC artists were not getting the exposure they deserved. They needed access to resources to help advance their talents as performing artists."

Banks emphasizes that VOCA provides year-round programming that everyone is welcome to enjoy. One popular program has been a paint-and-sip event held at the John F. Kennedy Center for the Performing Arts. Ongoing programs include workshops with other theater companies, as well as community engagement activities, such as VOCA's monthly cultural programs that aim to highlight diversity. They offer dance workshops in a variety of styles, including hip hop, modern, and African, and they run a summer camp for deaf and hard-of-hearing youth.

VOCA's theatrical performances take place at the Atlas Performing Arts Center. Originally built in 1938, the Atlas was one of four movie theaters in the District and it's now on the National Register of Historic Places. Its old-school marquee welcomes you inside its modern interior and four performance spaces. Atlas is at the center of a hub of cultural expression in Northeast DC.

Address 1333 H Street NE, Washington, DC 20002, +1 (202) 552-4687 (for hearing), +1 (202) 568-8864 (videophone), www.vocarts.org, info@vocarts.org | Getting there DC streetcar to 13th & H Streets NE; bus X2, X9, B2 to 14th & H Streets NE | Hours See website for performance schedule | Tip Anacostia Playhouse's mission is to bring arts performances, exhibits, and instruction to the Anacostia community, and to provide a venue for local artists to perform and display their work. Join them for one of their exciting performances (2020 Shannon Place SE, anacostiaplayhouse.com).

104__Washington Commanders

Catch the spirit at FedexField

2023 was a good year for the Washington Commanders. Fans were excited and energized by the National Football League (NFL) franchise's first new management team in 24 years, led by Josh Harris. NBA legend and hall of famer Magic Johnson is a new co-owner.

That same year, Jennifer King entered her third full season coaching in the NFL for the Commanders, and her third season as their assistant running backs coach after she was promoted to the role following the 2020 season. With the promotion, King became the first Black woman to hold a full-time position as a coach in NFL history.

Prior to coming to Washington, DC, King coached in the Alliance of American Football, and in the college ranks, and she also has experience as a player. From 2006-17 – seven seasons – King was an all-American quarterback and wide receiver for the Carolina Phoenix women's tackle football team.

Enjoy a day out at a Commanders home game at FedexField in Landover, MD, about five miles east of DC. The open-air stadium has five levels and seats about 60,000 spectators – with plenty of parking. One of the features at the stadium is the result of their "Command the Canvas" art initiative. Fifteen local artists from DC, MD and VA were selected from hundreds of applicants to create artwork that celebrates life in the area, the team history, and the excitement surrounding the inaugural season of the Washington Commanders.

King is enjoying DC. "I love DC. The culture and diversity make it a really fun city. I'm a history nerd, so I love the museums. The steps of the Lincoln Memorial are so peaceful at nighttime and have become a random go-to for me," she says. "You can't talk DC without talking food. I've been to so many great restaurants, but Stan's and Joe's Seafood, Prime Steak and Stone Crab are two of my favorites," says King.

Address 1600 Fedex Way, Landover, MD 20785, +1 (301) 276-6000, www.commanders.com | Getting there Metro to Morgan Boulevard (Blue, Silver Lines) | Hours Check website for game schedule | Tip Mamie "Peanut" Johnson was the first woman ever to pitch in baseball's Negro Leagues and was a longtime resident of Washington, DC. A new green space named in her honor at a once busy intersection hosts pedestrian-friendly walkways and bicycle lanes (New York & Florida Avenues NE, avenue-intersection.ddot.dc.gov).

105 The Washington Informer

Representing the Black community for over 50 years

Denise Rolark-Barnes is Publisher of *The Washington Informer*, a multimedia news organization and dominant force in delivering African American-related news and information to readers in DC, Maryland, and Virginia. *The Informer* was founded in 1965 by her father, Dr. Calvin W. Rolark, Sr. (1927–1994). His goal was to serve the Black community and to counter the racism that often appeared in the mainstream press, similar to that of *Freedom's Journal*, created in 1827 as the first Black-owned and operated newspaper in the US. You are welcome to pay a visit to the *Informer's* headquarters to see their operation and learn more about the history of the Black press in the United States.

Rolark-Barnes attended Howard University as an undergraduate. She later enrolled in Howard Law School and served as editor of the student newspaper *The Barrister*. Under her leadership, the *Informer* has continued to be cutting-edge and progressive. In 2023, Rolark-Barnes was named "Sales and Marketing Innovator of the Year" by the Local Media Association, a network of more than 3,000 newspapers, broadcasters, and related organizations.

People seek out *The Informer* for fresh perspectives on news and entertainment. "The COVID-19 pandemic and the death of George Floyd made a lot of people start focusing on things in our society that they had overlooked or taken for granted, like racial disparities, voting rights and even the Black media," Rolark Barnes said in an interview with *The Washington Post*. These are the issues that *The Informer* has been striving to address all along.

The Washington Informer also connects with readers by hosting tours around the metropolitan area for education and discovery, and by sponsoring the annual DC Citywide Spelling Bee for over 40 years, in which more than 2,000 elementary and middle school students participate.

Address 3117 Martin Luther King, Jr. Avenue SE, Washington, DC 20032, +1 (202) 561-4100, www.washingtoninformer.com | **Getting there** Bus A2, A4, A8, W1 to Martin Luther King, Jr. Avenue & 5th Street SE | **Hours** Mon–Fri 9am–5pm | **Tip** Open Crumb is a family-owned restaurant offering West African and American dishes, including a popular chicken sandwich, stews, jollof rice, *fufu*, mac & cheese, and much more (1243 Good Hope Road SE, www.opencrumbdc.com).

106 __ Washington National Cathedral

Stained glass windows representing justice for all

The Washington National Cathedral majestically towers over the nation's capital. In 1791, Pierre L'Enfant (1754–1825) envisioned a great church for national purposes. It wasn't until 1893 that Congress granted a charter to the Protestant Episcopal Cathedral Foundation of the District of Columbia, allowing it to establish a cathedral and institutions of higher learning.

The National Cathedral embraces diversity, welcoming everyone, and has made changes to demonstrate its commitment to inclusivity. In 2017, the cathedral removed two stained-glass windows featuring Robert E. Lee and Thomas "Stonewall" Jackson. "They celebrated the two generals, but they did nothing to address the reality and painful legacy of America's original sin of slavery and racism. They represented a false narrative of what America once was and left out the painful truth of our history," said The Very Rev. Randolph Marshall Hollerith, Dean of the Cathedral. "We're excited to share a new and more complete story, to tell the truth about our past and to lift up who we aspire to be as a nation."

In 2023, the *Now and Forever Windows* were dedicated. Designed by renowned artist Kerry James Marshall, they capture the resilience, faith, and endurance of African Americans. The original poem *American Song* by DC native Dr. Elizabeth Alexander is written beneath the windows. They are viewable in the nave, the central part of the Cathedral, on the main level.

"African American Voices" is a guided tour that explores the Black experience and notable contributions. You'll see the stone carving honoring Rosa Parks in the Human Rights Porch, a statue of the Rev. Martin Luther King, Jr., who preached his last Sunday Sermon here in 1968, and a needlepoint cushion honoring Harriet Tubman.

Address 3101 Wisconsin Avenue NW, Washington, DC 20016, +1 (202) 537-6200, www.cathedral.org, info@cathedral.org | Getting there Bus 31, 33, 96 to Woodley Road & Wisconsin Avenue NW | Hours See website for events and tour schedule | Tip Nearby Steak and Egg Diner has been serving up their hearty meals at reasonable prices to everyone from students to dignitaries since the 1930s. And if you're lucky, your meal will be delivered by their in-house robot (4700 Wisconsin Avenue NW, www.steakneggdiner.com).

107 Westminster Church

Jesus, justice, and jazz

Westminster Presbyterian Church is a hidden gem in the city. This progressive church has existed since 1853, and it has been in its current location since 1965. Rev. Brian Hamilton is the pastor of Westminster, which has hosted music programs for the past 25 years. "Jazz Night in DC" has become a local institution, taking place every Friday, while "Blue Monday Blues" concerts occur every Monday. Both events feature the finest DC-based performers. The concerts intentionally highlight jazz and blues in an effort to help preserve the rich historical legacy of DC's musical traditions. The jazz here is "straight-ahead," infused with a lot of swing, and the blues is mostly electric and Memphis-style.

Rev. Hamilton grew up in a small town in Maine, where his uncle gave him his first jazz album, Nina Simone's *High Priestess of Soul*. This gift introduced him to a bigger world than the one in which he grew up, and his love of jazz continued to grow. Rev. Hamilton closely co-organizes these music series with premiere jazz vocalist Dick Smith, who is also a former player for Washington's NFL team. They charge a small fee for tickets, and you can also enjoy a delicious and reasonably priced soul-food dinner. Come as you are, dressed up or down, and ready for a fun evening out.

"As a faith community, Westminster envisions a world where the justice, equity, and love taught by Jesus are lived and enjoyed by everyone," according to the church's website. Westminster's vision is evident in the events and programs that they offer. They are most recently working on a project to provide affordable housing to seniors and families. They've worked for justice from early support of the Freedmen's Bureau to leadership in anti-racism and the fight for LGBTQIA+ justice. The church also founded the well-known Food & Friends organization to provide meals to home-bound people with AIDS.

Address 400 I Street SW, Washington, DC 20024, +1 (202) 484-7700, www.westminsterdc.org | Getting there Metro to Waterfront (Green Line); bus P6 to 4th & I Streets SW | Hours See website for concert and events schedule | Tip Cane is a Michelin-rated Bib Gourmand restaurant specializing in Trinidadian street food served in a cozy, brightly colored, and stylish environment. The name references Trinidad's history of producing sugar cane. Former President Obama dined here (403 H Street NE, www.cane-dc.com).

108

The Whitelaw Hotel

The first luxury hotel for African Americans

Born in Virginia, John Whitelaw Lewis would become a member of Coxey's Army, the movement of jobless people who marched to DC in 1894 to protest unemployment during the worst economic depression until that time. Lewis marched barefoot, "with his shoes and belongings tied to a stick across his shoulders," reported William D. Nixon of *The Evening Star*.

It was then no small feat that Lewis, who worked his way up to become a prominent businessman and civic leader, later opened Industrial Bank, the first successful banking institution for Black people in Washington, DC. Lewis also envisioned a hotel to serve the needs of the Black community. "John was a dreamer, and it was within those dreams that he could envision a life that was outside his current economic condition to which he could aspire," notes James Louis Bacon in his book *Until I am Dust: The Story of the Industrial Bank and Whitelaw Hotel*. Lewis was able to encourage enough members of the Black community to buy $12 shares in the property in order to fund the hotel.

The Whitelaw Hotel opened in 1919 to great fanfare as the first hotel and apartment building financed, designed, built, and managed exclusively by Black Americans. The Whitelaw became a hub of social activity, and it boasted a large ballroom. This was one of the few places Black people could enjoy luxurious accommodations in the city during a time of racial segregation. It hosted well-known entertainers who performed on nearby Black Broadway, people moving to the city, and visitors from out of town. After desegregation and the 1968 riots, the hotel fell into decline. Fortunately, it was restored and reopened in 1992 with 1-to-3-bedroom apartments, and the ballroom was restored for resident activities and community events. You can admire the stunning Italian Renaissance revival style and architectural details on the exterior.

Address 1839 13th Street NW, Washington, DC 20009 Getting there Metro to U Street/
African American Civil War Memorial/Cardozo (Green Line); bus 90, 92, 96 to 13th &
U Streets NW; DC Circulator to 14th & U Streets NW (Woodley Park-Adams Morgan-
McPherson Square Line) Hours Unrestricted from the outside Tip After Reconstruction,
The True Reformer building was the first building in the United States to be designed, financed,
built, and owned by Black Americans. The True Reformers were an organization dedicated to
social change (1200 U Street NW, www.publicwelfare.org/true-reformer-building).

109

Williams Slave Pen Site

Acknowledging the cries of the enslaved

From 1836 to 1850, an unassuming, two-story, yellow house hid a horrific secret from the world outside. Inside its walls were imprisoned men, women, and children, who were held in chains, helpless and devoid of freedom for no other reason than the color of their skin. This notorious building was the Williams Slave Pen, owned by one W. H. Williams.

A slave pen was a holding place for enslaved Black people prior to their being sold at auction. They would then be held there until transportation was arranged to their next location. Washington was a strategic hub for these activities due to its proximity to waterways and railroads. The actual building and at least six similar ones that existed in the city no longer remain; however, a marker stands at this historic site to recount a part of the history of slavery in the American capital city.

The most well-known person subjected to the inhumane treatment in the Williams Slave Pen was Solomon Northup, who recounted his experience of being a free Black man sold into slavery in his autobiographical book, *Twelve Years a Slave: Narrative of Solomon Northup* (1853). "It was like a farmer's barnyard in most respects, save it was so constructed that the outside world could never see the human cattle that were herded there...," Northup wrote. "Strange as it may seem, within plain sight of this same house, looking down from its commanding height upon it, was the Capitol. The voices of patriotic representatives boasting of freedom and equality, and the rattling of the poor slave's chains, almost commingled."

As part of the Compromise of 1850, Congress sought to end the slave trade (but not slavery) and passed legislation to outlaw these types of prisons. The Williams Slave Pen closed shortly thereafter, although others continued to operate in nearby Alexandria, Virginia. The US Government unveiled two plaques on the site in 2017.

The Williams' Slave Pen

In 1841, Solomon Northup, a free Black man and professional musician, was drugged, kidnapped, and sold as a slave while visiting Washington, DC to attend the funeral of President William Henry Harrison. Eventually, Northup regained his freedom and documented the experience in his book, *Twelve Years a Slave: Narrative of Solomon Northup* (1853). The book includes a firsthand account of the Williams Slave Pen, where Northup was first imprisoned:

"The yard extended rearward from the house about thirty feet. In one part of the wall there was a strongly ironed door, opening into a narrow, covered passage, leading along one side of the house into the street. The doom of the colored man, upon who the door leading out of that narrow passage closed, was sealed. The top of the wall supported one end of a roof, which ascended inwards, forming a kind of open shed. Underneath the roof there was a crazy loft all round, where slaves, if so disposed, might sleep at night, or in inclement weather seek shelter from the storm. It was like a farmer's barnyard in most respects, save it was so constructed that the outside world could never see the human cattle that were herded there.

The building to which the yard was attached, was two stories high, fronting on one of the public streets of Washington, its outside presented only the appearance of a quiet private residence. A stranger looking at it, would never have dreamed of its execrable uses. Strange as it may seem, within plain sight of this same house, looking down from its commanding height upon it, was the Capitol."

This image of a Southwest DC slave pen is from a broadside published in 1836 by the American Anti-Slavery Society condemning the sale of humans into slavery.

Address Independence Avenue & 7th Street SW, Washington, DC 20591 | Getting there Metro to L'Enfant Plaza (Blue, Green, Orange, Silver, Yellow Lines); bus 33, 70, 74, S2 to 7th Street & Independence Avenue SW; DC Circulator to Jefferson Drive & 7th Street SW (National Mall Line) | Hours Unrestricted | Tip The DC Court of Appeals is housed in the old City Hall, Washington's first public building. Trials of abolitionists and Underground Railroad participants took place here in the early 1820s (430 E Street NW, www.dccourts.gov).

110 Woodlawn Manor Cultural Park

Discovering paths to freedom

A visit to Woodlawn Manor Cultural Park provides a better understanding of 19th-century life in this area of Montgomery County. From the 1830s to the 1860s, the residents were primarily farmers, enslaved people, free Black communities, abolitionists, and Quakers. A guided tour on the Underground Railroad (UGRR) Experience Trail takes you on a historic journey to hear stories about the people who lived here and about the experiences of freedom seekers on the UGRR. Or you can pick up a self-guided map in the Visitors Center to experience the trail at your own pace.

The park recounts the story of William Palmer, a farmer, physician, and Quaker who relocated here from Pennsylvania in 1815 and purchased the 24-acre estate in 1822. After the death of his first wife, Martha, he married his second wife, Cleora DuVall who was not a Quaker. She brought 12 enslaved people into the marriage.

The park is owned and operated by the MD-National Capital Park & Planning Commission. In 2016, a museum was established in a historic, 1832 barn, covering the history of the area and its residents through a combination of visual and audio presentations. On the self-guided tour, you can explore three levels of the restored barn, where you'll view farming implements, read stories of enslaved and free families in the area, and experience audio and video presentations about life at Woodlawn.

Although it is believed that there was UGRR activity in this area, there was none on the path you will follow that was established in 1998. The guides interpret challenges and strategies that would have been used by those seeking freedom. While you're here, you can also view the manor house where the Palmers lived and an original log cabin that may have been used as housing for enslaved persons.

Address 16501 Norwood Road, Sandy Spring, MD 20860, +1 (301) 929-5989, www.montgomeryparks.org/parks-and-trails/woodlawn-manor-cultural-park | Getting there By car, take Georgia Avenue north, turn right onto Layhill Road and left onto Norwood Road | Hours Daily dawn–dusk | Tip Enjoy southern comfort food at Miss Toya's Creole House, serving blackened salmon, jambalaya, and bayou rolls made with diced chicken and vegetables wrapped in a crispy egg roll and served with creole aioli (923 Ellsworth Drive, Silver Spring, MD, www.misstoyascreolehouse.com).

111 The Wormley Hotel

History worth noting of a famous hotel

A marker is all that remains of the prestigious Wormley Hotel. At one time the most successful and expensive hotel in Washington, DC, it catered to the nation's most prominent visitors and residents.

James Wormley (1819-1884) was born free near the White House to parents Lynch and Mary Wormley. Lynch started a successful carriage business with his sons as drivers to provide transportation for politicians, socialites, and businessmen. As he drove government leaders around in his carriage, Wormley was exposed to sensitive information and came to be trusted for maintaining confidentiality. He constantly nurtured his relationships with the most powerful people in the city, and he received training in the art of being a host. The family had been able to acquire several properties with assistance from his connections, and Wormley opened his hotel and restaurant business during the 1850s.

The five-story Wormley Hotel offered a bar, a barbershop, and an acclaimed dining room, where Wormley served European-style dishes using fresh ingredients he grew on his nearby farm. Within Gore Vidal's historical novel *1876*, the character Miss Augustine Snead says, "Most European royalty stay at Wormley's Hotel. Why haven't you, Princess?"

The hotel was also the site of the "Wormley Agreement," the name given to the Compromise of 1877 that ended the intensely disputed presidential election of 1876. Rutherford B. Hayes would be the president, leading to the end of Reconstruction in the South.

James Wormley was an advocate for education, and he was instrumental in the creation of the Sumner School, the city's first public elementary school for Black children. He died after a surgical procedure in Boston, and many of Washington's major hotels lowered their flags to half-staff in tribute. His sons ran the hotel for another decade, and then sold the business.

Wormley's Hotel Site

1500 H Street, NW

James Wormley (1819–1884), free-born like his parents, was one of a number of African American entrepreneurs with downtown hospitality and service businesses. His five-story Wormley's Hotel opened here in 1871, catering primarily to a wealthy and politically powerful white clientele. It hosted the "Wormley Hotel conference," at which representatives of Republican Rutherford B. Hayes and Democrat Samuel J. Tilden brokered a deal over the contested presidential election of 1876. This "Compromise of 1877" led to Hayes assuming the Presidency, the removal of troops from the South and the end of federal Reconstruction. Wormley's son sold the hotel in 1893, and Union Trust Bank replaced it in 1906.

Address 1500 H Street NW, Washington, DC 20005 | Getting there Metro to McPherson Square (Blue, Orange, Silver Lines); bus 11Y, 32, 33, 36 to 15th Street & New York Avenue NW | Hours Unrestricted | Tip Wormley family's estate site is gone, but you can go find a historic marker on the site where it once stood that tells the family's story (3530 Van Ness Street NW, www.culturaltourismdc.org).

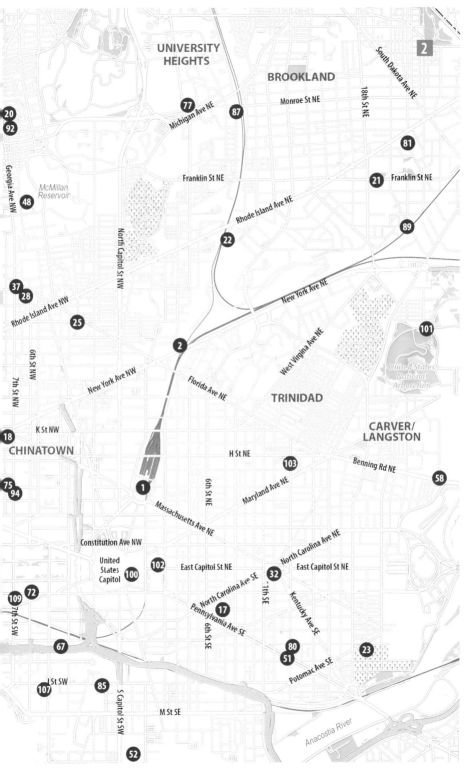

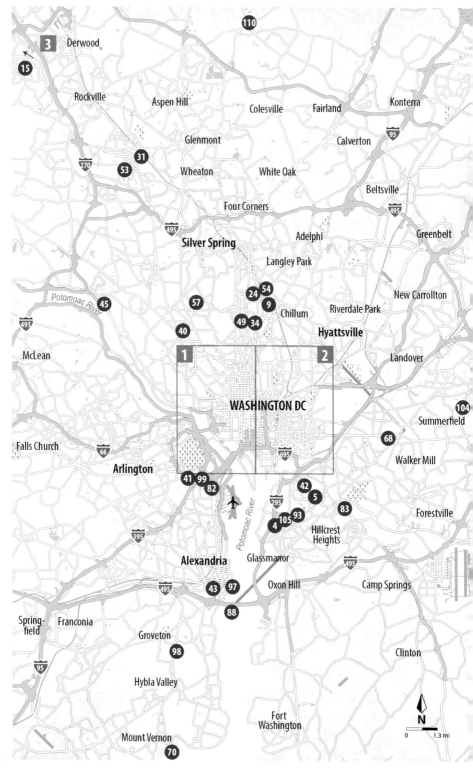

Andrea Seiger, John Dean
111 Places in Washington
That You Must Not Miss
ISBN 978-3-7408-1890-6

Kaitlin Calogera, Rebecca Grawl,
Cynthia Schiavetto Staliunas
111 Places in Women's
History in Washington
That You Must Not Miss
ISBN 978-3-7408-1590-5

Allison Robicelli, John Dean
111 Places in Baltimore
That You Must Not Miss
ISBN 978-3-7408-1696-4

Jo-Anne Elikann, Susan Lusk
111 Places in New York
That You Must Not Miss
ISBN 978-3-7408-1888-3

Wendy Lubovich, Ed Lefkowicz
111 Museums in New York
That You Must Not Miss
ISBN 978-3-7408-0379-7

Wendy Lubovich, Jean Hodgens
111 Places in the Hamptons
That You Must Not Miss
ISBN 978-3-7408-1891-3

Kim Windyka, Heather Kapplow,
Alyssa Wood
111 Places in Boston
That You Must Not Miss
ISBN 978-3-7408-1558-5

Brandon Schultz, Lucy Baber
111 Places in Philadelphia
That You Must Not Miss
ISBN 978-3-7408-1376-5

Brian Hayden, Jesse Pitzler
111 Places in Buffalo
That You Must Not Miss
ISBN 978-3-7408-1440-3

Amy Bizzarri, Susie Inverso
111 Places in Chicago
That You Must Not Miss
ISBN 978-3-7408-1030-6

Michelle Madden, Janet McMillan
111 Places in Milwaukee
That You Must Not Miss
ISBN 978-3-7408-1643-8

Sandra Gurvis, Mitch Geiser
111 Places in Columbus
That You Must Not Miss
ISBN 978-3-7408-0600-2

Philip D. Armour, Susie Inverso
111 Places in Denver
That You Must Not Miss
ISBN 978-3-7408-1220-1

Cristyle Egitto, Jakob Takos
111 Places in Palm Beach
That You Must Not Miss
ISBN 978-3-7408-1695-7

Floriana Petersen, Steve Werney
111 Places in San Francisco
That You Must Not Miss
ISBN 978-3-7408-2058-9

Floriana Petersen, Steve Werney
111 Places in Napa and Sonoma
That You Must Not Miss
ISBN 978-3-7408-1553-0

Floriana Petersen, Steve Werney
111 Places in Silicon Valley
That You Must Not Miss
ISBN 978-3-7408-1346-8

Harriet Baskas, Cortney Kelley
111 Places in Seattle
That You Must Not Miss
ISBN 978-3-7408-1992-7

National Museum of African American Art (ch. 73): Installation photography from "Visionary: Viewpoints on Africa's Arts," November 4, 2017 to ongoing, NMAfA_2017_Visionary_029, National Museum of African Art, Smithsonian Institution (upper); Skirt - Zulu artist, ca. 1950s, Leather, cloth, glass and plastic beads, metal tacks, fiber, H x W x D: 73.5 x 93.2 x 4.5 cm (28 15/16 x 36 11/16 x 1 3/4 in.), 99-4-1, Museum purchase (lower), National Museum of African Art, Smithsonian Institution (lower)

Curls (ch. 74): Sonya Clark, *Curls,* 2005; Plastic combs, 96 x 36 x 36 in.; Museum purchase: Members' Acquisition Fund and Belinda de Gaudemar Acquisition Fund;

Queen City Sculpture (ch 84): Nekisha Durrett, Artist;© Sonya Clark

The Last Supper (ch. 91): Akili Ron Anderson, Artist

I am forever grateful to those who helped bring this book to fruition. First, I thank God for divine guidance. Thanks to publisher Emons Verlag for agreeing with my vision of a culturally focused guide, making this the first of its kind in their collection, along with editor Karen Seiger for her thoughtful guidance and support. I value the key information and memories from fellow DC explorers Paige Muller, Monica Malouf, and Andrea Seiger, along with those from family and friends old and new whom I spoke with along this journey. And my eternal love to my parents Carrie and Rev. Donald Nichols Sr., incredible role models, who always supported my dreams.

Lauri Williamson is a licensed tour guide and entrepreneur. She grew up in New Jersey, moved to Washington to attend Howard University and fell in love with the city. She enjoys creating experiences that both educate and enlighten visitors to DC.

David Wardrick, Digital Storyteller, is a lifelong resident of the Washington, DC region, where he focuses on visual media production. He is an award-winning photographer and videographer with four decades of production experience. David's work has been featured in *USA Today*, NASA-TV, multiple books, magazines, and across social media. He has a passion for the history of the nation's capital.

The information in this book was accurate at the time of publication, but it can change at any time. Please confirm the details for the places you're planning to visit before you head out on your adventures.